HANDMADE PASTA WORKSHOP & COOKBOOK

HANDMADE PASTA WORKSHOP & COOKBOOK

RECIPES, TIPS & TRICKS FOR MAKING PASTA BY HAND, WITH PERFECTLY PAIRED SAUCES

NICOLE KARR

PAGE STREET
PUBLISHING CO.

PAGE STREET
PUBLISHING CO.

Copyright © 2016 Nicole Karr

First published in 2016 by
Page Street Publishing Co.
27 Congress Street, Suite 105
Salem, MA 01970
www.pagestreetpublishing.com

Distributed by Macmillan, sales in Canada by The Canadian Manda Group.

19 18 17 16   1 2 3 4 5

ISBN-13: 978-1-62414-322-9
ISBN-10: 1-62414-322-9

Library of Congress Control Number: 2016940930

Cover and book design by Page Street Publishing Co.
Photography by Christina Sico

Printed and bound in the United States

Page Street is proud to be a member of 1% for the Planet. Members donate
one percent of their sales to one or more of the over 1,500 environmental and
sustainability charities across the globe who participate in this program.

GRANDMA ROSIE. I'D TRADE IT ALL
FOR JUST ONE DAY TO COOK WITH YOU.

CONTENTS

Introduction   9

PART I: THE BASICS   10
PASTA MAKING WORKSHOP AND DOUGH RECIPES   11
Equipment   12
Ingredients   13
How to Make Pasta Dough   15
Dough Recipes   19

PART II: THE RECIPES   22
PASTA BY HAND   23
Fusilli with Roasted Cauliflower and Anchovies   25
Whole Wheat Cavatelli with Mushrooms and Goat Cheese Crema   27
Frascatelli with Sweet Corn Carbonara   31
Ricotta Cavatelli with Mussels   32
Pici with Black Pepper, Pecorino and Guanciale   35
Capunti with Crispy Calamari, Kale and Burrata   36
Malloreddus with Juniper Berry Braised Venison   39
Cecamariti with Figs, Pancetta and Brussels Sprouts   42
Black Pepper Trofie with Clams, Fennel and Sausage   45
Lorighittas with Heirloom Tomatoes, 'Nduja and Oil-Cured Olives   47
Orecchiette and Meatballs   51
Maccheroni di Busa with Brasciole and Pomodoro Sauce   54
Gnocchetti with Fava Beans, Shrimp and Pistachio Pesto   57
Ciciones with Lentil Stew   60
Casarecce with Crispy Artichokes, Lemon and Scamorza   63
Mezzi Paccheri with Peas and Onions   65
Strozzapreti with Green Tomatoes and Crab   69

GNOCCHI AND GNUDI 71

Egg Yolk Gnudi with Truffles — 72

Pumpkin Gnocchi with Pancetta and Swiss Chard Pesto — 75

Sweet Potato Gnocchi with Pecans and Prosciutto — 76

Ramp Gnudi and Grana Padano — 79

Beet Gnocchi with Sheep's Milk Ricotta and Sage — 80

Saffron Gnocchi with Butter Poached Lobster and Tarragon — 83

Roasted Potato Gnocchi with Robiola, Artichokes and Capers — 85

Crispy Lemon Gnocchi with Sweet Peas and Scallops — 89

Chickpea Gnudi with Heirloom Tomatoes — 90

Gnocchi Verdi with Provolone Fonduta — 93

STUFFED PASTA 95

Polenta Raviolo with Guanciale and Wild Mushrooms — 96

Eggplant Mezzaluna with Tomato Confit and Pesto — 99

Butternut Squash and Roasted Pear Cappellacci with Sage — 101

Veal Agnolotti with Mustard Greens and Pecorino — 105

Prosciutto Caramelle with Gorgonzola Fonduta — 107

Anolini in Brodo — 111

Sweet Pea Raviolini with Mascarpone and Mint — 112

Espresso Braised Short Rib and Celery Root Ravioli — 115

Radicchio and Taleggio Triangoli with Pork Cheek Ragu — 116

Sunchoke Cappelletti with Kale and Apples — 121

Faggotini with Dill, Shrimp and Zucchini — 122

Artichoke Casonsei with Hazelnuts and Goat's Milk Ricotta — 125

Pork and Parsnip Tortelli with Apples and Walnuts — 126

Beet and Rose Scarpinocc with Poppy seeds — 129

Culurgiones with Brown Butter and Almonds — 132

CUT PASTA

CUT PASTA 135

Roasted Garlic Fettuccine with Razor Clams and Baccala 136

Farfalle with Roasted Tomatoes and Chile 139

Tagliatelle Primavera 142

Ink Spaghetti alla Chitarra with Cured Yolk and Poached Egg 145

Pappardelle with Wild Mushroom Bolognese 147

Cocoa Mafaldine with Quail and Walnuts 151

Herb Fettuccine with Mussels and Speck 152

Pizzoccheri with Swiss Chard, Fingerlings and Grana Padana 155

Tagliarini with Cerignola Olives and Lemon 156

Spaghetti Cacio e Pepe 159

Chestnut Stracci with Braised Pork Ribs and Pears 160

Herb Garganelli with Artichokes and Meyer Lemon 163

Cappellacci dei Briganti with Eggplant Caponata 164

Ink Farfalle with Octopus, Calabrian Chiles and Chickpeas 167

Mint Corzetti with Lamb Sausage and Broccoli Rabe 168

Herb Fazzoletti with Tuna and Castelvetrano Olives 171

Sorprese with Roasted Butternut Squash and Hazelnuts 172

BAKED PASTA

BAKED PASTA 175

Ratatouille Lasagna 176

Eggplant Cannelloni 179

Spinach and Taleggio Rotolo 180

Escarole and Sausage Cannelloni 183

Grandma Rosie's Timballo 184

About the Author 186

Acknowledgments 187

Index 188

INTRODUCTION

Whether you grew up on a rustic farm in Tuscany or in a close-knit Italian family in Queens, waking up every Sunday to the sizzle of meatballs hitting a cast-iron skillet for Grandma Rosie's Sunday dinner, you know the evocative comfort and tradition of Italian cooking. Even if you didn't grow up this way, we all know the enveloping warmth and magnetic pull of the love of food and cooking it.

The fact is, so many of us who "live to eat" instead of "eating to live" have many memories and traditions revolving around the dinner table that have shaped our lives. The idea of "working with what you've got" is a constant inspiration in the kitchen. One of my favorite examples of this is a folk tale about the origin of tiramisu. In my favorite version of this story, a soldier's wife is preparing dessert from the meager rations in the kitchen during World War II and lovingly layers stale bread with stale biscuits and softens it by soaking it in coffee for her family: tiramisu was born. Food is love, and necessity breeds invention.

As a chef, my career has brought me to so many different places and introduced me to an array of cuisines, but none resonated with me as much as Italy and my time spent there making pasta. In Italy, the local traditions vary from region to region, city to city and family to family. Pasta making is so rich in tradition and history, I became infatuated with it. I dedicated all of my time to learning every shape and noticed that the same pasta shape goes by a different name in another town, punctuated only by a difference in the length or the twist of the dough. Today, my love affair with pasta continues, and I take every opportunity I can to expose people to its beautiful history.

My grandma Rosie's Sunday dinner tradition is the deep connection I feel between the way I was raised and the cultural tradition of fresh food being at the center of our lives. I don't enjoy the theatrical display of science and showmanship that is molecular gastronomy, the newest haute cuisine trend. Instead, I prefer the enduring simplicity of fresh ingredients prepared with love. Tastes change, palates change, the availability of ingredients changes, and the pioneering human spirit that adapts and improves and compounds these rich traditions, dish by dish, is the inspiration for this book and for my life in the kitchen.

Nicole K

CHAPTER ONE

PASTA MAKING WORKSHOP AND DOUGH RECIPES

Why on earth would anyone sit around making pasta by hand when there's a pot of water and a box of spaghetti five feet away? I am a firm believer in the cathartic powers of making pasta by hand, kneading the dough, adding flour and water as needed, getting your hands dirty as a means of creating something tasty and beautiful. I also believe that making pasta by hand is not nearly as hard as you undoubtedly think it is, or as time consuming.

This chapter is a tutorial of sorts; once you master these hard and fast "rules" of the basic dough we use in all the pasta recipes in the book, the rest is gravy. I urge you to make the dough in this chapter as written first, and to take off from there once the process of mixing, kneading, resting and rolling becomes familiar to you; it will get ingrained into your muscle memory faster than you think.

This isn't a workshop intended to dispel the myths of a buxom Italian nonna covered in flour, simultaneously marrying off her eldest daughter and saying a rosary. It is, instead, a crash course of sorts in the basic dough-making process we use in the dumpling, pasta by hand, cut and baked pasta recipes throughout the book. There's no need to buy out the complicated pasta tool section of a department store before beginning the learning process of pasta by hand. This book will grow with you as you master more and more of the recipes, techniques and shapes outlined in the following chapters.

EQUIPMENT

Most pastas in the book can be made with tools you already have in your kitchen. Some of the specialty tools described below are standard in any Italian kitchen; as you continue to explore your own culinary prowess, consider adding these to your kitchen toolbox:

BENCH SCRAPER
Tool used to manipulate dough and aid in the kneading process.

CHITARRA
Italian for guitar, although it has an almost harp-like appearance. A rolled sheet of pasta dough is placed to fit over the wires and a pin is rolled over with light pressure to cut into strands.

CORZETTI STAMP
A special carved wooden hand tool that produces thin rounds of pasta that are given an embossed decoration.

CAVAROLA BOARD
A traditional wooden board from Italy's Mezzogiorno region, used to press a pattern into the pasta.

DIGITAL SCALE
Essential in ensuring accurate and consistent measurements.

DRYING RACK
Used to dry out semolina-based pastas.

GNOCCHI/GARGANELLI BOARD
These flat boards have a rigid surface and are used to create grooves in the pasta, which hold the sauce and create texture.

PASTRY WHEEL
There are two types of pastry wheels that can be used to cut pasta dough: one with a straight edge and one with a jagged edge perfect for making a zigzag design.

PASTA MACHINE/SHEETER
A pasta machine is used to roll out the dough into sheets. The rollers on the machine adjust to multiple thickness settings. Most machines come with an attachment that will also cut the sheets into fettucine or spaghetti.

PASTA EXTRUDER
This machine will automatically mix and knead pasta dough, then extrude it under very high pressure through dies to form the desired pasta shape.

POTATO RICER
Used to mash potatoes to a smooth and fluffy consistency. Perfect when making gnocchi.

ROLLING PIN
The old-school way of rolling out sheets of dough. This is typically how it is done in Italy. If you have one of these, you too can make handmade pasta!

PIPING BAG
Piping bags are the best way to neatly and evenly distribute fillings into your pasta. If you don't have access to a piping bag, you can fill a plastic bag with the filling and just cut the tip off.

PASTRY BRUSH
Can be used to brush dough with water to aid in the sealing of stuffed pasta or to clean pasta-making equipment.

RAVIOLI STAMP
Used to cut and seal ravioli:

SCOOP
A scoop is a great tool to help ensure even and consistent measurements.

SPRAY BOTTLE
Essential in evenly incorporating water into the dough to add moisture.

INGREDIENTS

Basic pasta dough consists of two very simple ingredients: flour and water. Understanding and mastering the principles of pasta making will allow you to get creative and turn the dough into endless flavor and texture possibilities. It is important to remember: You will make mistakes along the way! These fumbles through the trial-and-error process are invaluable in your mastery of pasta making.

FLOUR
Typically, pasta dough can be divided into two distinctive categories: pasta made with 00 flour (or doppio zero) and eggs and pasta made with durum semolina flour and water.

Wheat flour is the main ingredient in pasta and can be classified as either "soft" or "hard." The anatomy of a kernel of wheat consists of three components: the bran, which is the outer layer of the kernel; the endosperm, which is the largest portion; and the germ, which is the smallest portion of a wheat kernel and is the part from which new plants germinate. The milling and sifting out of the germ and bran in soft wheat leaves you with the endosperm, which results in fine, powdery flour. Most Italian flours are graded with numbers to indicate the fineness of the grind.

One of the most finely ground soft wheat flours is 00 flour. It contains far less gluten and more starch than other flours. It is an ideal pasta-making flour to create a soft and delicate bite. It's usually used when making stuffed pastas and different types of cut pastas (tagliatelle, pappardelle, etc.). You can find 00 flour in any specialty Italian market or online. If you can't find it, it is perfectly fine to use all-purpose flour. Just remember that the benefits of using 00 flour are a silkier and softer pasta.

When whole durum wheat is milled, the endosperm resists breaking, and the resulting flour is a coarse, granular flour called semolina. Semolina flour, a type of "hard" wheat, is rich in gluten and makes for a more textured and dense pasta. It is the main component when making both extruded pasta (rigatoni, spaghetti, bucatini) and hand-formed pastas made with semolina dough (orecchiette, gnocchetti, cavatelli).

WATER

The water component of the dough could be any type of liquid (water, eggs, olive oil, vegetable purees). Without some type of hydrating component, the gluten in the wheat will never form and you won't have a dough. With too little, you're looking at a crumbly mess; with too much, you'll have a sticky blob. As you move through the process of making pasta by hand, you will strike this balance. It's also important to remember that this is an ever-changing chemical formula. Outside elements such as temperature and humidity will change the structure of the dough. For example, high humidity will affect how much moisture is absorbed into the flour. Be mindful that cooking is one part fundamentals and one part intuition. I like to think of cooking like jazz: we know the basic chord structure and use our natural intuition, experience in the kitchen, and general whimsy to add the top notes. If the dough feels too dry, you can add some water. The best way to control the dough's moisture level is with a spray bottle of water. One small spritz often really brings the dough together.

When selecting eggs for pasta dough, I like to use eggs straight from the farmers market whenever possible. Eggs laid by free-range chickens have the richest yolks and yield the best dough. Eggs also enhance the color and texture of the pasta, so it's vital that you select the freshest ingredients whenever you can. Egg whites add protein and water, and the yolks add protein and fat, which weaken the dough and make it more tender. In Italy, the yolk of the egg has a deep red-orange color and is called red (rosso) instead of yellow. That's what gives Italian pasta its rich yellow color and tender bite. However, if you don't have the option to walk out of your Tuscan villa to your rustic Italian garden and reach up under your prized chicken and grab an egg for your pasta, always go with the freshest ingredients available to you.

SALT

When salt is added to any dough, it will tighten up the dough and the gluten will become stronger. This is essential when making pasta that will be heavily manipulated by hand. It will ensure that the dough can withstand rolling, stretching and shaping and give it the consistency necessary not to fall apart. You will find in my recipes that I always use kosher salt. Unlike table salt, kosher salt has a much larger and coarser grain, which makes the salt easier to hold and control when seasoning.

HOW TO MAKE PASTA DOUGH

For many, the thought of "making" pasta is a daunting and fearsome Everest they may never climb. And, oh my, the mess. Most people feel that only a professional chef can (or should) do it. To those people I say emphatically, You are wrong! Making fresh pasta by hand is a very intimate and enjoyable process anyone can master. As with everything else, practice makes perfect in pasta making. The reward that comes from making a complete meal entirely from scratch far outweighs the pitfalls and fumbles in the beginning while we figure it out. Understanding the ingredients that are used to make pasta dough and how they react when combined is crucial in making a successful dough.

MEASURING

In this book, my recipes use one of two forms of measurement: volume (cups) and weight (grams). I highly recommend adding a digital scale to your kitchen arsenal if you don't have one already. Using a digital scale is really the best way to ensure precise and accurate measures, which guarantees consistency in the kitchen. If you choose to use measuring cups, be sure to scoop, pack in and level off any excess ingredient as accurately as possible.

MIXING

There are many ways to go about mixing pasta dough. It is pretty much a matter of preference. Mixing can be done in the bowl of a stand mixer or in a food processor. I like to mix my dough by hand on a wooden surface.

To mix by hand, dump the flour on a dry work surface and form a mound about 10 inches (25.4 cm) in diameter. Using your hands, create a well in the middle of the flour mound. Slowly pour the wet ingredients into the middle and gradually work the flour in using your fingers or a fork. Combine the flour and wet ingredients until fully incorporated. (If you find that the dough is too dry, spray some water onto it with your spray bottle. If it is sticking to the surface, sprinkle some flour on the dough.)

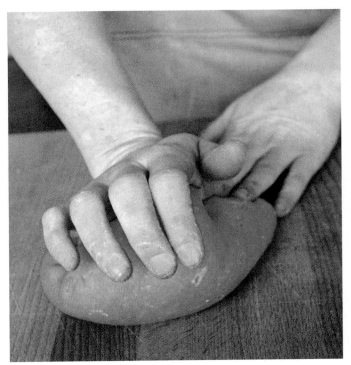

To knead, push down with the heel of your hand.

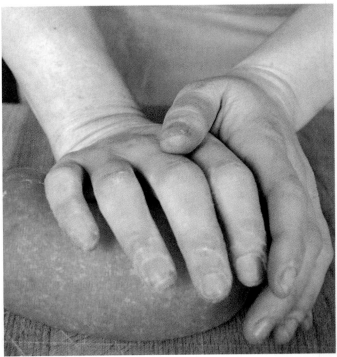

Rotate the dough as you knead it.

Dough should have a smooth texture when sufficiently kneaded.

Allow the dough to rest for at least 30 minutes before using.

KNEADING

Once the ingredients of the dough have come together, begin to knead it by pushing down on the dough with the heel of your hand and rotating it. Knead your dough for at least 10 to 15 minutes. When the dough has had been sufficiently kneaded, it will have stopped changing appearance and will have a smooth surface. Keep in mind that it is almost impossible to overknead pasta dough (carpal tunnel is a more likely outcome) but very easy to underknead it. It may feel like it is taking forever, but making pasta dough is a labor of love requiring patience and perseverance. Wrap the dough tightly in plastic wrap and allow to rest. (See photos to left.)

RESTING

This is one of the most important steps in making fresh pasta dough, and, I have found, in life. During the resting period, gluten is given a chance to form and the dough gains elasticity. Without sufficient resting time, the dough will resist rolling and stretching, which makes the remainder of this process unnecessarily difficult. It is best to let the dough rest for at least 30 minutes at room temperature if you intend to use it right away. After 30 minutes, the dough should be refrigerated. Pasta dough is best when used within 24 hours, but it may be stored in the freezer for up to a month.

ROLLING AND SHAPING

Before you start rolling out any dough, it is crucial for it to be at room temperature and to be well rested. If you are using a dough that has been refrigerated, allow it to reach room temperature by letting it sit out for about 30 minutes.

The process of rolling the dough is essentially the same whether you are doing it with a rolling pin, a hand-cranked pasta machine or an electric machine.

To roll using a machine, cut off a piece of dough and rewrap the unused dough with plastic wrap. If you don't wrap the dough, the air will start to dehydrate the dough and make it unusable. Place the dough on a dry work surface, and with a rolling pin start to flatten it until it is able to fit into the widest setting of the pasta machine. Feed the dough through the machine at the widest setting, passing it through twice. Reduce rollers to the next narrowest setting, and pass the dough through. Continue to pass the dough through the machine, changing the settings each time until you have reached the desired thickness for the pasta you are making. Be sure to gradually change the settings as you roll; making the dough too thin too fast will cause it to tear and bunch up. For the most part, dough will be rolled out to around $\frac{1}{16}$ inch (1.6 mm) thick. The finished dough should be slightly translucent.

To roll out the dough using a rolling pin, place the dough on a lightly floured surface and begin rolling the dough using a gentle back and forth motion, rotating it every so often and lifting the dough off of the work surface to prevent it from sticking. As a general rule of thumb, I like to roll the dough into the shape of pasta I'm making. If I am making round corzetti, I roll the dough into a circle. Tailoring the shapes to the dough right off the bat creates less waste and makes your life easier.

Most hand-formed pasta requires no rolling out at all. It is easily shaped by hand, and, for me, the most fun to make.

STORING AND COOKING

The ingredients in the pasta you make determine the best way they should be stored. Semolina-based pastas can be dried out and stored at room temperature because they contain only flour and water.

When making any type of stuffed pasta, I find it best to freeze the pasta before cooking. If you think about it, the wet filling is encased by delicate, moisture-absorbing sheets of dough. If you refrigerate it, the pasta will become soggy and limp. Freezing the pasta before you cook it ensures the pasta won't fall apart, and it doesn't affect the time that it needs to be cooked. The only exception to my rule is when making pasta stuffed with ricotta cheese. I find with ricotta, the cheese will become grainy after cooking if it has been frozen, so it is best to cook ricotta-stuffed pasta right away after making. The best way to freeze pasta is to just stick the whole sheet pan in the freezer. Once the pasta is partially frozen, you can use it right away or transfer it to a freezer-safe zip bag where it can be stored frozen for up to a month.

The boiling of any pasta should be done in a pot large enough to let it move freely in generously salted (as salty as the sea) water. There are no set rules regarding cooking times, as all pastas are unique. As a general rule, the pasta should be cooked al dente ("to the tooth"). The best way to test that is to taste it. It's that simple. If you were to cut a piece of al dente pasta in half, you would see a white core, which is often referred to as "the soul of the pasta." Pasta that is being tossed with a sauce should be cooked only about 90 percent of the way, as it will continue to cook while in the pan.

USING THE RECIPES

Pasta has a varied, assorted, debatable and deep-rooted history. None of the recipes in this book are to be considered "traditional." These recipes are my own interpretation of classic dishes. I encourage anyone cooking from this book to make the recipes your own. Don't go crazy searching for an ingredient if it's not in season or if you can't find it. Substitute and tweak. Use your own sense of taste and experience to tailor the recipes to you and your family. However, substitutions in classic dishes must make sense. For example, using ziti and adding heavy cream to a carbonara makes no sense; it is no longer a carbonara. But if you use bucatini instead of spaghetti and pancetta instead of guanciale, that makes sense.

Another important rule when cooking is to always taste your food at every step. It is perhaps the biggest untold and obvious secret when it comes to cooking and is often not mentioned in recipes. Additionally, season each recipe the way you like it. If you like your sauce a little spicy, add another pinch of crushed red pepper. Cooking is all about being creative and doing what feels right.

DOUGH RECIPES

The following dough recipes are what I like to refer to as my "master doughs." Each dough can be used as a base to expand on once you are comfortable making it.

EGG DOUGH

This rich all-yolk dough makes for beautiful, delicate and silky noodles. Perfect for any pasta that won't be manipulated too much.

YIELDS 1 LB 7 OZ (650 G)

2 cups (254 g) 00 flour

1 tsp (5 g) kosher salt

20 egg yolks

2 tsp (10 ml) extra-virgin olive oil

To make the Egg Dough, mix the 00 flour and salt on a dry work surface. Form a mound about 10 inches (25 cm) in diameter.

Using your hands, create a well in the middle of the flour-and-salt mixture. Slowly pour the egg yolks and oil into the middle and gently beat. Gradually work the flour in using your fingers or a fork. Combine the flour, egg yolks and oil until fully incorporated. If the dough is sticking to your work surface, add a little bit of flour. If the dough feels dry, spray a little bit of water to bind it together.

Once the dough is formed into a ball, begin to knead it by pushing down with the heel of your hand and rotating it. Knead the dough for about 10 to 15 minutes. The dough has had sufficient kneading when it has a smooth appearance and springs back when you press it.

Wrap the dough tightly with plastic wrap and let it rest for at least 30 minutes at room temperature before using. If you are not using the dough right away, refrigerate it.

RAVIOLI DOUGH

The whole eggs in this recipe provide the protein necessary to make this dough strong enough to be rolled out thin and twisted into the desired shape. Perfect for any stuffed pasta shapes.

YIELDS 2 LB (908 G)

4 cups (508 g) 00 flour

1 tsp (5 g) kosher salt

5 eggs

6 egg yolks

To make the Ravioli Dough, mix the 00 flour and salt on a dry work surface. Form a mound about 10 inches (25 cm) in diameter.

Using your hands, create a well in the middle of the flour-and-salt mixture. Slowly pour the eggs and egg yolks into the middle and gently beat. Gradually work the flour in using your fingers or a fork. Combine the flour and eggs until everything is fully incorporated. If the dough is sticking to your work surface, add a little bit of flour. If the dough feels dry, spray a little bit of water to bind it together.

Once the dough is formed into a ball, begin to knead it by pushing down with the heel of your hand and rotating it. Knead the dough for about 10 to 15 minutes. The dough has had sufficient kneading when it has a smooth appearance and springs back when you press it.

Wrap the dough tightly with plastic wrap and let it rest for at least 30 minutes at room temperature before using. If you are not using the dough right away, refrigerate it.

SEMOLINA DOUGH

Semolina dough is essential in making shapes like orecchiette, pici and gnocchetti. Most of the boxed pastas you see in grocery stores contain the very same ingredients. Semolina-based pastas are perfect for drying because they contain no eggs, which also makes them great for vegans.

YIELDS 1 LB (454 G)

1 cup (168 g) semolina flour

1 cup (127 g) 00 flour

1 tbsp (10 g) kosher salt

¾ cup (178 ml) warm water

To make the Semolina Dough, combine the flours and salt and place on a dry work surface. Form a mound about 10 inches (25 cm) in diameter. Using your hands, create a well in the middle of the flour-and-salt mixture. Slowly pour the water into the middle and gradually work the flour in using your fingers or a fork. Combine the flour and water until it all is fully incorporated. If the dough is sticking to your work surface, add a little bit of flour. If the dough feels dry, spray a little bit of water to bind it together.

Once the dough is formed into a ball, begin to knead it by pushing down with the heel of your hand and rotating it. Knead the dough for about 10 minutes. The dough has had sufficient kneading when it has a smooth appearance and springs back when you press it.

Wrap the dough tightly with plastic wrap and let it rest for at least 30 minutes at room temperature before using. If you are not using the dough right away, refrigerate it.

EXTRUDED DOUGH

Extruded dough is not like all the others. Forget what you learned about all the rules of dough making for this recipe. A crumbly consistency like wet sand is essential in ensuring that the dough will withstand the extruding process. Once you are comfortable with using an extruder, the dough possibilities and shapes are endless.

YIELDS 1 LB (454 G)

2 cups (336 g) semolina flour

½ cup (118 ml) warm water

To make the Extruded Dough, place the semolina flour in the base of the extruder. With the mixer running, slowly start to pour the water into the base with the flour. The dough is ready to be extruded when it resembles wet sand. It will look crumbly and should stick together when pressed between your fingers. Extrude the pasta according to the manufacturer's directions for the machine or attachment.

CHAPTER TWO

PASTA BY HAND

Making pasta by hand is the most richly satisfying, intimate and rewarding thing I do as a chef. Over the years, I've found that the hypnotic repetition of shaping pasta by hand, as well as the catharsis associated with a job well done, is as close to Zen as I've come since my Play-Doh days. Remember: every pasta made by a pasta machine was first formed by hand. Whether you're a seasoned pasta chef or a weekend warrior getting their feet wet, I urge you to use this time in the kitchen to connect to your home and hearth and start your own traditions as I have in the spirit of craftsmanship. If you're looking for the least labor-intensive chapter in this book, look no further. Pasta by hand is the most forgiving and most interpretive of those in the book.

FUSILLI WITH ROASTED CAULIFLOWER AND ANCHOVIES

"Fusilli" is derived from the Italian *fuso* or "spun," and these little corkscrew pasta ribbons are just that. Their coiled shape is perfect for capturing every bit of sauce. The lemon adds the perfect balance against the salty anchovies and roasted cauliflower.

SERVES 4–6

FUSILLI
Semolina Dough (page 21)

ROASTED CAULIFLOWER
1 large cauliflower, cut into small pieces

Olive oil

1 garlic clove, thinly sliced

Crushed red pepper, to taste

Kosher salt

Freshly ground black pepper

RUSTIC BREAD CRUMBS
1 loaf fresh Italian bread, cut into ½-inch (12-mm) pieces

Olive oil

1 tsp dried Italian seasoning

¼ cup (45 g) grated Parmigiano-Reggiano

TO FINISH
Olive oil

1 (1.6-oz [45-g]) can anchovies, roughly chopped

1 lemon, juice and zest

Parsley, chopped

Preheat the oven to 400°F (204°C) and dust two sheet pans with semolina flour.

To make the fusilli, cut off a small piece of Semolina Dough and cover the rest of the dough with plastic wrap. Roll the piece of dough into a rope about ¼-inch (6-mm) thick. Cut 2½-inch (6.4-cm) pieces of dough from the rope. Place a piece of cut dough on a diagonal and place the skewer at the bottom end of the piece of dough, then roll the skewer away from you until the dough is all wrapped around it. Do not press hard or the dough will stick to the skewer. Gently slide the pasta off the skewer and place on the semolina-dusted sheet pan. Leave uncovered until ready to cook.

Toss the cut pieces of cauliflower in a bowl with olive oil, sliced garlic, crushed red pepper, salt and freshly ground black pepper. Place on a sheet pan and bake for about 25 minutes or until tender.

For the bread crumbs, place cut Italian bread onto sheet pan and drizzle with olive oil, dried Italian seasoning, grated Parmigiano-Reggiano, salt and freshly ground black pepper. Bake for about 10 minutes or until crusty. Place the bread in a food processor and pulse until just ground.

Bring a large pot of salted water to boil.

In the meantime, in a large sauté pan over medium heat, add a drizzle of olive oil, chopped anchovies, cauliflower and lemon juice. Stir to combine and keep warm while pasta cooks.

Drop the fusilli in the boiling water and cook until al dente, about 4 to 5 minutes. Add the fusilli to the sauté pan with the cauliflower and toss to combine. Season with salt and freshly ground pepper.

To serve, divide the pasta between bowls. Garnish with lemon zest, bread crumbs and chopped parsley.

(continued)

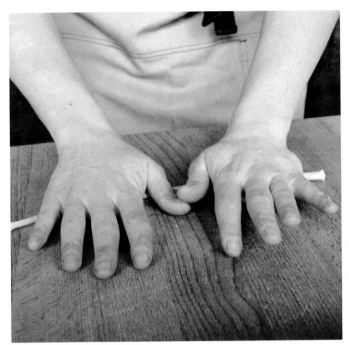

Roll the dough into a rope about a ¼-inch (6-mm) thick.

Wrap the rope around the skewer.

Allow the fusilli to dry a few minutes and then carefully remove skewer.

Finished fusilli.

WHOLE WHEAT CAVATELLI WITH MUSHROOMS AND GOAT CHEESE CREMA

This hearty Cavatelli stands up perfectly to the earthy flavor of the mushrooms. The crema adds a perfect balance of richness and can be substituted with the robust soft cheese of your choice.

SERVES 4–6

WHOLE WHEAT CAVATELLI

1 cup (168 g) semolina flour

1 cup (120 g) whole wheat flour

1 tbsp (10 g) kosher salt

¾ cup (178 ml) warm water

GOAT CHEESE CREMA

8 oz (227 g) goat cheese

¼ cup (59 ml) heavy cream

TO FINISH

Olive oil

1 bulb fennel, thinly sliced, reserve fronds for garnish

1½ lb (680 g) wild mushrooms

Kosher salt

Freshly ground black pepper

1 cup (237 ml) white wine

Dust two sheet pans with semolina flour.

To make the dough, follow the instructions for Semolina Dough (page 21). To make the cavatelli, cut off a small piece of whole wheat dough and cover the rest of the dough with plastic wrap. With your hands, roll the piece of dough into a rope about ½-inch (12-mm) thick. Cut 1-inch (2.5-cm) pieces of dough from the rope. Using a butter knife or bench scraper, push down firmly on the edge of the dough and drag the knife away from you, allowing the dough to curl over on itself. Place the cavatelli on the semolina-dusted sheet pan and leave uncovered until ready to cook.

To make the goat cheese crema, in a bowl, add the goat cheese and heavy cream. Whisk until well combined and smooth.

In a large sauté pan over high heat, add a drizzle of olive oil, fennel, wild mushrooms, salt and freshly ground pepper. Cook for about 6 minutes or until the fennel and mushrooms are caramelized, stirring frequently. Add white wine and let it reduce by half.

Bring a large pot of salted water to a boil. Drop the cavatelli in the boiling water and cook to al dente, about 4 to 5 minutes. Add the cavatelli to the sauté pan with the caramelized fennel and mushrooms. Toss to combine.

To serve, divide the pasta between bowls. Garnish with goat cheese crema and fennel fronds.

(continued)

Roll the dough into a rope about ½-inch (1.3-cm) thick and cut it into 1-inch (2.5-cm) pieces.

Using a bench scraper, push down firmly on the edge of the dough.

Drag the bench scraper away from you allowing the dough to curl over.

Finished cavatelli.

FRASCATELLI WITH SWEET CORN CARBONARA

This recipe is my personal take on carbonara. The sweetness of the corn balances the richness of the lardo for a hearty dish with a satisfying finish. While it's a perfect pairing with a pork chop or seared scallops, I prefer to eat it alone and savor the creaminess of this dish with the bite of the frascatelli.

SERVES 4–6

FRASCATELLI

2 cups (472 ml) water

4 cups (672 g) semolina flour

CORN MILK

3 cups (711 ml) whole milk

1 bunch thyme

4 corn cobs, kernels removed and reserved

3 eggs

SAUTÉED CORN

Olive oil

¼ cup (58 g) unsalted butter

3 leeks, sliced

Kosher salt

Freshly ground black pepper

TO FINISH

¼ lb (113 g) lardo, cut into ¼-inch (6-mm) pieces

½ cup (90 g) grated Parmigiano-Reggiano

Chives, thinly sliced

To make the frascatelli, fill a bowl with cold water. Line a sheet pan with parchment paper and place the semolina flour on another sheet pan. Dip your fingertips into the water and allow the water droplets to fall onto the pan with semolina. Using a bench scraper, carefully turn the semolina over onto itself to create irregular pebble-size pieces of dough. Using the bench scraper, transfer the semolina flour with the dough pieces into a sieve. Gently shake the sieve, allowing the semolina to fall back onto the sheet pan and leaving the frascatelli. Transfer the frascatelli to the parchment-lined sheet pan. Continue the process until very little semolina remains. Place the frascatelli in the freezer until ready to use. This ensures that the pasta won't fall apart during cooking.

In a medium-size pot, over medium-low heat, add the whole milk, thyme and cobs. Bring to a simmer and allow to cook for about 30 minutes. Discard the cobs and pass the milk through a sieve. Allow the milk to cool and then add the eggs and whisk until well combined.

Bring a large pot of salted water to a boil.

In a large sauté pan over high heat, add a drizzle of olive oil, butter, corn, leeks, salt and freshly ground pepper. Cook for about 5 minutes, stirring frequently, until soft. Reduce heat to low.

Drop the frascatelli in the boiling water and cook until they float, about 1 to 3 minutes.

Add the frascatelli and lardo to the sauté pan with the corn and leeks. Toss to combine, and remove from heat. Slowly, and stirring constantly, start to incorporate the egg-and-milk mixture to the pan until it thickens, about 2 minutes. Add the grated Parmigiano-Reggiano and toss to combine.

To serve, divide the pasta between bowls. Garnish with chives and freshly ground black pepper.

RICOTTA CAVATELLI WITH MUSSELS

Another "hearty bite" dish, the salty mussels balance the creamy cheese in this recipe, which is great for any season.

SERVES 4–6

RICOTTA CAVATELLI

1 cup (227 g) ricotta

1½ cups (191 g) 00 flour

2 eggs

Kosher salt

Freshly ground black pepper

STEAMED MUSSELS

Olive oil

1 shallot, sliced

1 garlic clove, chopped

1 bulb fennel, halved, sliced, fronds reserved

Crushed red pepper, to taste

3 lb (1.4 kg) mussels, scrubbed

1 lemon, juice and zest

¼ cup (59 ml) dry vermouth

¼ cup (58 g) unsalted butter

Kosher salt

Freshly ground black pepper

TO FINISH

1 loaf Italian bread, sliced

Olive oil

Ricotta

Dust two sheet pans with semolina flour.

To make the dough, combine the ricotta, flour, eggs, salt and freshly ground pepper in a bowl. Mix together until well incorporated and place on a lightly floured work surface. Knead for about 5 minutes. To make the cavatelli, cut off a small piece of ricotta dough and cover the rest with plastic wrap. With your hands, roll the piece of dough into a rope about ½-inch (12-mm) thick. Cut 1-inch (2.5-cm) pieces of dough from the rope. Using a butter knife or bench scraper, push down firmly on the edge of the dough and drag the knife away from you, allowing the dough to curl over on itself. Place the cavatelli on the floured sheet pan and leave it uncovered in the refrigerator until ready to cook.

Bring a large pot of salted water to a boil.

To steam the mussels, in a pot over high heat, add a drizzle of olive oil, shallot, garlic, fennel and crushed red pepper. Cook for about 2 minutes or until soft. Then add the mussels, lemon juice, zest, vermouth, butter, salt and freshly ground pepper. Cover and cook until the mussels open, about 3 to 5 minutes

In the meantime, drop the cavatelli in the boiling water and cook until they float, about 2 to 4 minutes. Drizzle the sliced Italian bread with olive oil and broil in the oven for about 1 minute on each side or until toasted.

Add the cavatelli to the mussels and stir to combine.

To serve, divide the pasta and mussels between bowls. Garnish with a slice of crusty Italian bread, olive oil, fennel fronds and a few small dollops of ricotta.

PICI WITH BLACK PEPPER, PECORINO AND GUANCIALE

This is as traditional and rustic a pasta shape as there is, hailing from southern Tuscany. The long, thick, and irregular length of the pasta makes it a perfect match for thick and hearty sauces, as in this smoky, meaty dish.

SERVES 4–6

PICI

Semolina Dough (page 21)

TO FINISH

1 lb (454 g) guanciale, cut into ½-inch (12-mm) pieces

Olive oil

Freshly ground black pepper

Pecorino Romano, for grating

Dust two sheet pans with semolina flour.

To make the pici, cut off a small piece of semolina dough and cover the rest of the dough with plastic wrap. With your hands, roll the piece of dough into a rope about ¼-inch (6-mm) thick. Cut 6-inch (15-cm) pieces of dough from the rope. It is normal for pici to be irregular lengths and thickness. Place the pici on the semolina-dusted sheet pan and leave it uncovered until ready to cook.

Bring a large pot of salted water to a boil.

In the meantime, in a large sauté pan over medium-high heat, cook the guanciale until crispy and the fat is rendered out, about 5 minutes. Drop the pici in the boiling water and cook until al dente, about 3 to 5 minutes. Add the pici to the guanciale and toss to combine.

To serve, divide the pici between bowls. Garnish with a drizzle of olive oil, freshly ground black pepper and grated Pecorino Romano.

CAPUNTI WITH CRISPY CALAMARI, KALE AND BURRATA

This empty "pea pod" is a shape typical of Puglia and very similar to cavatelli. The capunti provide a perfect vessel for capturing every bit of sauce and have a nice bite to them.

SERVES 4–6

CAPUNTI

Semolina Dough (page 21)

CRISPY CALAMARI

Vegetable oil, for frying

1 cup (125 g) all-purpose flour

1 cup (168 g) semolina flour

1 cup (170 g) cornmeal

Kosher salt

1 lb (454 g) calamari, cut into ½-inch (12-mm) rings

TO FINISH

Olive oil

2 garlic cloves, sliced

2 lb (907 g) kale

Kosher salt

Freshly ground black pepper

¼ lb (113 g) burrata

Italian flat-leaf parsley, chopped

1 lemon, juice and zest

Dust two sheet pans with semolina flour.

To make the capunti, cut off a small piece of Semolina Dough and cover the rest with plastic wrap. With your hands, roll the piece of dough into a rope about ½-inch (12-mm) thick. Cut 2-inch (5-cm) pieces of dough from the rope. Using three fingers, push down firmly on the dough, dragging it across the work surface toward your body. Place the capunti on the semolina-dusted sheet pan and leave it uncovered until ready to cook.

Bring a large pot of salted water to a boil.

To make the crispy calamari, heat oil in a pot or a deep fryer to 400°F (204°C). In a bowl, combine the all-purpose flour, semolina, cornmeal and salt. Working in batches, dredge the calamari in the dry mixture, shaking off the excess before you drop it into the heated oil. Fry until golden brown, about 2 minutes. Remove from the oil and place on a paper towel–lined sheet pan. Season with salt.

Drop the capunti in the boiling water and cook until al dente, about 3 to 5 minutes

In the meantime, in a sauté pan over medium-high heat, add a drizzle of olive oil, garlic and kale. Season with salt and freshly ground black pepper. Add the cooked capunti and toss to combine.

To serve, divide the pasta between plates. Add some of the crispy calamari to each bowl and garnish with burrata, chopped parsley, olive oil, lemon juice and zest.

(continued)

Roll the dough into a rope about ½-thick (12-mm) and cut into 2-inch (5-cm) pieces.

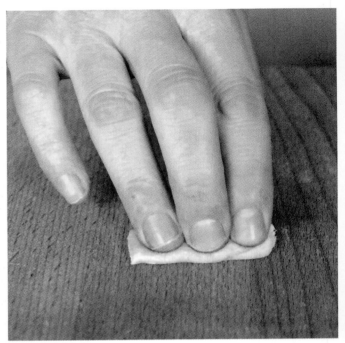

Using your fingers, push down firmly on the dough.

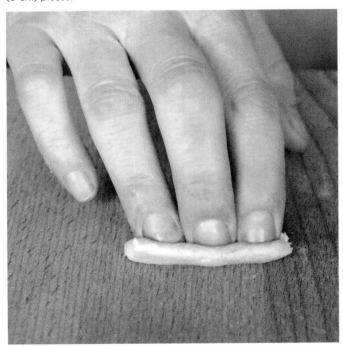

Drag the dough across your work surface toward your body.

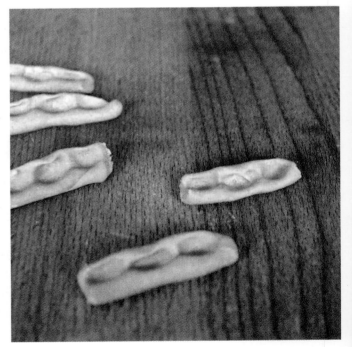

Finished capunti.

MALLOREDDUS WITH JUNIPER BERRY BRAISED VENISON

This Sardinian pasta staple balances a tiny, delicate pasta shape with the hearty venison. In another happy accident, making this dish is a form of aromatherapy guaranteed to call your friends and family—and neighbors—to the table *subito*.

SERVES 4–6

BRAISED VENISON

Olive oil

4 lb (1.8 kg) venison shoulder or shank

Kosher salt

Freshly ground black pepper

1 carrot, diced

1 stalk celery, diced

2 onions, diced

1 garlic clove, chopped

3 tbsp (48 g) tomato paste

1 cup (237 ml) red wine

3 cups (711 ml) beef stock

3 sprigs thyme

1 bay leaf

1 tsp juniper berries

MALLOREDDUS

Semolina Dough (page 21)

TO FINISH

Kosher salt

Freshly ground black pepper

Italian flat-leaf parsley, chopped

Preheat oven to 350°F (177°C). To braise the venison, heat a large Dutch oven with olive oil over high heat. Season venison generously with salt and freshly ground pepper. Add the venison to the pan and cook until brown, about 2 to 3 minutes per side. Remove the venison and set aside. Reduce the heat to medium and add the carrot, celery, onions and garlic and cook until they begin to brown, about 5 minutes. Add the tomato paste and cook for about 2 minutes, stirring frequently so it doesn't burn. Add the red wine, beef stock, thyme, bay leaf and juniper berries and bring up to a boil. Return the venison to the pot and cover. Place it in the oven and cook for about 1½ hours or until the meat is tender.

To make the malloreddus, dust 2 sheet pans with semolina flour and set aside. Cut off a small piece of Semolina Dough and cover the rest of the dough with plastic wrap. With your hands, roll the piece of dough into a rope about ½-inch (12-mm) thick. On a slight bias, cut ½-inch (12-mm) pieces of dough from the rope. With your thumb, apply pressure to just the top half of the piece of pasta with the side of your thumb, and press and push toward the bottom of a cheese grater. Place the malloreddus on the semolina-dusted sheet pans and leave it uncovered until ready to cook.

When the venison is cooked, remove it from the pot and strain the braising liquid. Discard the vegetables and herbs. Over medium heat, simmer the braising liquid until it has reduced by more than half and has thickened. Shred the venison and add it back to the pot with the braising liquid. Keep warm.

Bring a pot of salted water to boil. In the meantime, in a large sauté pan over low heat, add a drizzle of olive oil and some of the braised venison. Drop the pasta in the boiling water and cook until al dente, about 4 to 6 minutes. Add the cooked pasta and some of the pasta water to the venison. Toss to combine and season with salt and freshly ground black pepper. To serve, divide the pasta and venison between bowls. Garnish with chopped parsley.

(continued)

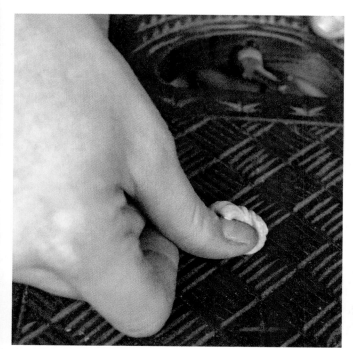

Roll a ½-inch (12-mm) cut piece of dough over a cavarola board or cheese grater.

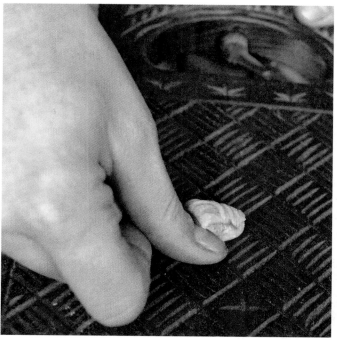

With your thumb, apply pressure to the top of the dough and press downward.

Finished malloreddus.

CECAMARITI WITH FIGS, PANCETTA AND BRUSSELS SPROUTS

Cecamariti, often referred to as "husband blinders," hail from the Lazio region. The story is that husbands would come home from working in the fields and would be blinded by how delicious these little spindle pastas are. Fresh figs are the perfect sweet companion to the salty pancetta. This definitely hits all the sweet and salty spots.

SERVES 4–6

CECAMARITI

1 tsp (4 g) instant yeast

½ cup (118 ml) warm water

⅛ cup (15 g) wheat flour

¾ cup (95 g) 00 flour

½ tsp (3 g) kosher salt

BRUSSELS SPROUTS

Olive oil

8 oz (227 g) pancetta, cut into ½-inch (12-mm) cubes

1 lb (454 g) Brussels sprouts, halved

3 garlic cloves, sliced

Kosher salt

Freshly ground black pepper

TO FINISH

16 black mission figs, quartered

¼ cup (43 g) chopped hazelnuts, toasted

Balsamic vinegar

Dust two sheet pans with 00 flour.

To make the dough, combine the yeast and warm water in a bowl and let sit for about 5 minutes. Then add the flours and salt to the bowl and mix until the dough just comes together. Allow the dough to sit for about 15 minutes, covered. On a lightly floured surface, gently knead the dough. Return the dough to an oiled bowl and cover. Let the dough sit for about 1 hour.

To make the cecamariti, cut off a small piece of dough and cover the rest of the dough with plastic wrap. With your hands, roll the piece of dough into a rope about ½-inch (12-mm) thick. Cut ½-inch (12-mm) pieces of dough from the rope. Using your fingers, begin rolling the piece back and forth until it is about 2 inches (5 cm) long and has a spindle-like shape. Place the cecamariti on the flour-dusted sheet pan and leave it uncovered until ready to cook.

Bring a large pot of salted water to boil.

To roast the Brussels sprouts, in a large sauté pan over high heat, add a drizzle of olive oil, the pancetta, Brussels sprouts and garlic and season with salt and freshly ground black pepper. Sauté until tender; keep warm.

Drop the cecamariti into the boiling water and cook until they float, about 1 to 3 minutes. Add to the pan with the Brussels sprouts and toss to combine.

To serve, divide the pasta between bowls. Garnish with figs, hazelnuts and a drizzle of balsamic vinegar.

BLACK PEPPER TROFIE WITH CLAMS, FENNEL AND SAUSAGE

This twisted Ligurian pasta, most often served with a pesto sauce, is deconstructed in this unique take on the dish with hearty sausage and a light clam flavor for the finish.

SERVES 4-6

BLACK PEPPER TROFIE

Semolina Dough (page 21)

2 tbsp (12 g) freshly ground black pepper

TO FINISH

Olive oil

1 bulb fennel, halved, thinly sliced

3 garlic cloves, chopped

1 shallot, sliced

8 oz (227 g) sweet Italian sausage, removed from casing

4 lb (1.8 kg) littleneck clams

1 lemon, juice and zest

1 cup (237 ml) white wine

¼ cup (58 g) unsalted butter

Kosher salt

Freshly ground black pepper

Dust two sheet pans with semolina flour.

To make the black pepper dough, follow the instructions for Semolina Dough, incorporating the black pepper with the dry ingredients.

To make the trofie, cut off a small piece of black pepper dough and cover the rest of the dough with plastic wrap. With your hands, roll the piece of dough into a rope about ¼-inch (6-mm) thick. Cut ½-inch (12-mm) pieces of dough from the rope. With your hands, one at a time, roll the pieces into ropes about ⅛-inch (3-mm) thick and 3 inches (7.6 cm) long. Using the side of your hand or a bench scraper positioned at an angle to the dough, push down firmly on the edge and drag toward your body. This will give the trofie its spiral shape. Place the trofie on the semolina-dusted sheet pans and leave it uncovered until ready to cook.

Bring a large pot of salted water to a boil.

To steam the clams, in a pot over high heat, add a drizzle of olive oil, fennel, garlic and shallot. Cook for about 2 minutes or until soft. Add the sausage, breaking it up in the pot. Cook until golden brown. Then add the clams, lemon juice, zest, white wine, butter, salt and freshly ground pepper. Cover and cook until the clams open, about 5 to 7 minutes.

In the meantime, drop the trofie in the boiling water and cook until al dente, about 1 to 3 minutes. Add the pasta to the pot with the mussels and stir to combine.

To serve, divide the pasta and clams between bowls.

(continued)

Roll the dough into a rope about ¼-inch (6-mm) thick and cut it into ½-inch (12-mm) pieces

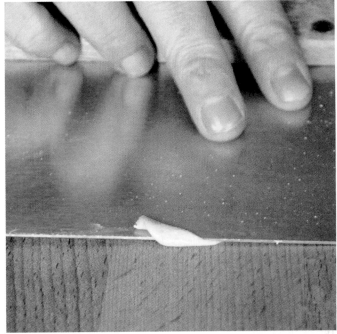

Using the side of your hand or a bench scraper, push down firmly on the edge of the dough and drag it toward you.

This will give the trofie its spiral shape.

Finished trofie.

LORIGHITTAS WITH HEIRLOOM TOMATOES, 'NDUJA AND OIL-CURED OLIVES

Named for the iron ring that was used to tether horses to hitching posts in old-time Sardinia, this unique pasta shape is offset by the spicy 'nduja and salty olives for a wildly gratifying pasta dish.

SERVES 4–6

LORIGHITTAS
Semolina Dough (page 21)

TO FINISH
Olive oil

8 oz (227 g) heirloom tomatoes, cut into pieces

1 garlic clove, thinly sliced

4 oz (113 g) 'nduja

Kosher salt

Freshly ground black pepper

¼ cup (45 g) oil-cured black olives, pitted and chopped

Basil

Dust two sheet pans with semolina flour.

To make the lorighittas, cut off a small piece of dough and cover the rest with plastic wrap. With your hands, roll the piece of dough into a rope about 1⁄16-inch (1.5-mm) thick. With your hands, wrap the rope around three fingers (index, middle, ring) on your right hand twice. Pinch the wrapped dough so it adheres to itself. Now, with the dough around your fingers, begin weaving it together to create a twisted braid. Place the lorighittas on the semolina-dusted sheet pans and leave it uncovered until ready to cook.

Bring a large pot of salted water to a boil.

In the meantime, in a large sauté pan over medium-high heat, add a drizzle of olive oil, tomatoes and garlic. Cook for about a minute. Stir in the 'nduja and break it up until it melts. Lower the heat to low and keep warm.

Drop the pasta in the boiling water and cook until al dente, about 3 to 4 minutes. Add the pasta to the pan with the tomatoes and toss to combine. Season with salt and freshly ground black pepper.

To serve, divide the pasta between bowls. Garnish with chopped olives and basil.

(continued)

LORIGHITTAS WITH HEIRLOOM TOMATOES, 'NDUJA AND OIL-CURED OLIVES (CONT.)

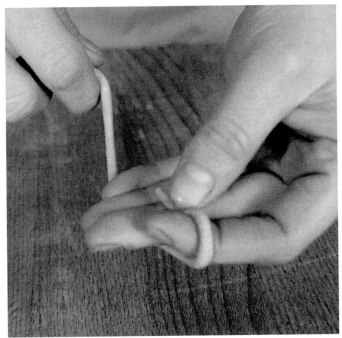

Roll the dough into a rope about 1/16-inch (1.5-mm) thick. Wrap the dough around three fingers twice.

Begin weaving the rope together.

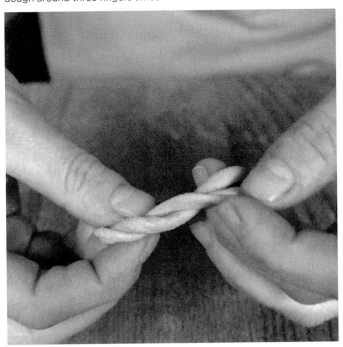

It should begin to resemble a twisted braid.

Finished lorighittas.

ORECCHIETTE AND MEATBALLS

Orecchiette is a hand-shaped pasta unique to the region of Puglia, located on the southeastern coast of Italy. Its name is derived from its shape, which resembles a small ear. I first learned to make orecchiette during my stay in Otranto under the tutelage of three Italian matrons while attending a school at "La Fattoria" (the farm) Agritourism. If I didn't shape it right, the misshapen pasta was thrown into a reject pile, and I was shamed. I was given disapproving looks again and again until I did it the right way. I paired this dish with meatballs to complement the natural bite of the pasta.

SERVES 4–6

ORECCHIETTE

Semolina Dough (page 21)

TOMATO SAUCE

Olive oil

3 garlic cloves, chopped

1 cup (237 ml) red wine

2 (28-oz [794-g]) cans crushed tomatoes

1 bunch basil

Kosher salt

Freshly ground black pepper

MEATBALLS

8 oz (227 g) ground beef

8 oz (227 g) ground veal

8 oz (227 g) ground pork

2 eggs

½ cup (60 g) bread crumbs

1 cup (180 g) grated Parmigiano-Reggiano

1 bunch Italian flat-leaf parsley, chopped

2 garlic cloves, minced

Crushed red pepper, to taste

Kosher salt

Freshly ground black pepper

2 slices white bread

TO FINISH

Parmigiano-Reggiano, for grating

Olive oil

Basil, torn

Preheat the oven to 400°F (204°C) and dust two sheet pans with semolina flour.

To make the dough, follow the instructions for Semolina Dough. To make the orecchiette, cut off a small piece of dough and cover the rest of the dough with plastic wrap. With your hands, roll the piece of dough into a rope about ½ inch (12 mm) wide. Cut ½-inch (12-mm) pieces of dough from the rope. Using a butter knife, push down firmly on the edge of the dough and drag the knife toward you. As the dough curls over the knife, use your thumb to uncurl the dough and make a dome shape (little ears). Place the orecchiette on the sheet pan and leave it uncovered until ready to cook.

To make the sauce, in a pot on medium heat, add the olive oil and garlic and sauté for about a minute or until translucent. Add the red wine and let it reduce by half. Then add the crushed tomatoes, basil, salt and pepper. Let it simmer on low while you make the meatballs.

(continued)

ORECCHIETTE AND MEATBALLS (CONT.)

To make the meatballs, in a large bowl mix the ground beef, veal, pork, eggs, bread crumbs, Parmigiano-Reggiano, parsley, garlic, crushed red pepper, salt and pepper. Soak 2 slices of white bread in water and squeeze out any excess. Add bread to the bowl and mix very well. Using your hands, shape the mixture into 1-inch (2.5-cm) balls. They should be a little smaller than a golf ball. Place on a pan and bake uncovered for about 15 minutes. Add the meatballs to the sauce and continue to simmer for about 30 minutes.

Bring a large pot of salted water to a boil. Drop the pasta in the boiling water and cook to al dente, about 3 minutes.

In a sauté pan, add a drizzle of olive oil, the pasta, meatballs and some tomato sauce. Toss to combine.

To serve, divide the pasta between bowls with meatballs. Garnish with freshly grated Parmigiano-Reggiano, olive oil and basil.

Roll the dough into a rope about ½-inch (12-mm) thick and cut it into ½-inch (12-mm) pieces.

Using a butter knife, push down firmly on the edge of the dough and drag the knife toward you.

Use your thumb to uncurl the dough and create a dome shape.

Finished orecchiette.

MACCHERONI DI BUSA WITH BRASCIOLE AND POMODORO SAUCE

This Sicilian dish is of the stick-to-your-ribs variety, fortified by the flavorful meat in the pomodoro sauce. The word *busa* derives from the Arabic word *bus*, the name of a plant, whose stem was used for both the making of pasta and knitting.

SERVES 4–6

MACCHERONI DI BUSA

Semolina Dough (page 21)

POMODORO SAUCE

Olive oil

3 garlic cloves, chopped

1 onion, diced small

2 lb (907 g) tomatoes, chopped

1 bunch basil

Kosher salt

Freshly ground black pepper

BRASCIOLE

2 lb (907 g) beef brasciole (top round steaks), pounded thin

Ground black pepper

1 cup (180 g) grated Parmigiano-Reggiano

1 bunch Italian flat-leaf parsley, chopped

Toothpicks or kitchen twine

TO FINISH

Parmigiano-Reggiano, for grating

1 bunch basil, torn

Dust two sheet pans with semolina flour.

To make the dough, follow the instructions for Semolina Dough. To make the maccheroni di busa, cut off a small piece of dough and cover the rest of the dough with plastic wrap. With your hands, roll the piece of dough into a rope about ½ inch (12 mm) wide. Cut 2-inch (5-cm) pieces of dough from the rope. Using a wooden skewer, place it down in the middle of the dough and pinch the dough to seal around the skewer. Using your palm with even pressure, roll back and forth to seal the dough and create a tube-like shape. Place the pasta on the sheet pan and leave it uncovered until ready to cook.

To make the sauce, in a pot on medium heat, add the olive oil, garlic and onion and sauté for about a minute or until translucent. Then add the chopped tomatoes, basil, salt and freshly ground black pepper. Allow the sauce to simmer on low while you make the brasciole.

To make the brasciole, lay the meat down on a cutting board and pound out evenly. Generously sprinkle pepper, Parmigiano-Reggiano and parsley over each piece, leaving about ¼ inch (6 mm) around the edges. Starting at one end, begin to tightly roll the meat. Secure with a toothpick or tie with kitchen twine. In a large sauté pan, drizzle olive oil and sear the brasciole on all sides until brown. Add the browned brasciole to the saucepot and allow it to simmer for at least 1 hour.

Bring a large pot of salted water to a boil. Drop the pasta in the boiling water and cook to al dente, about 3 minutes.

In a sauté pan, add a drizzle of olive oil, the pasta and some tomato sauce. Toss to combine.

To serve, divide the pasta between bowls with brasciole. Garnish with freshly grated Parmigiano-Reggiano and basil.

(continued)

Roll the dough into a rope about ½-inch (12-mm) thick and cut into 2-inch (5-cm) pieces. Place a wooden skewer in the middle of the cut piece.

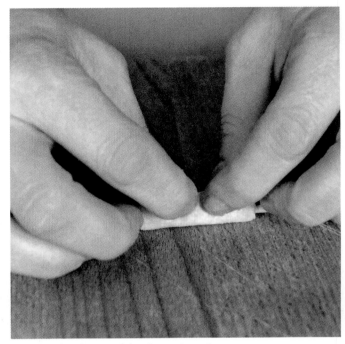

Pinch the dough around the skewer to seal.

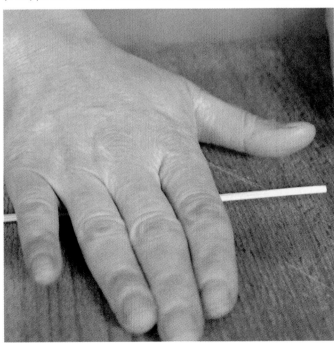

Using your palm, apply even pressure and roll back and forth. Carefully remove the skewer.

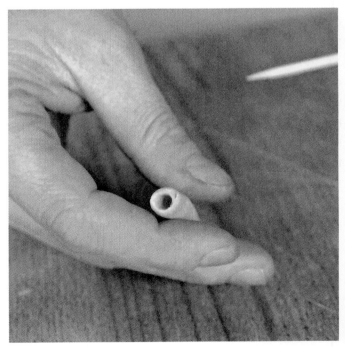

Finished maccheroni di busa.

GNOCCHETTI WITH FAVA BEANS, SHRIMP AND PISTACHIO PESTO

These hearty gnocchetti are the perfect complement to the delicate spring flavors of the shrimp and fava beans.

SERVES 4–6

GNOCCHETTI
Semolina Dough (page 21)

PISTACHIO PESTO
1 cup (150 g) pistachios

1 bunch mint

1 garlic clove

½ cup (50 g) grated Pecorino Romano

½ cup (118 ml) olive oil

Kosher salt

Freshly ground black pepper

TO FINISH
8 oz (227 g) fava beans

Olive oil

3 garlic cloves, chopped

2 lb (907 g) large shrimp, cleaned

Crushed red pepper, to taste

Kosher salt

Freshly ground black pepper

¼ cup (59 ml) white wine

1 lemon, zested

Dust two sheet pans with semolina flour.

To make the gnocchetti, cut off a small piece of dough and cover the rest of the dough with plastic wrap. With your hands, roll the piece of dough into a rope about ½-inch (12-mm) thick. Cut ½-inch (12-mm) pieces of dough from the rope. With your thumb, gently push the piece of dough onto a gnocchi board, rolling it away from your body so it creates a slight indentation. Place the gnocchetti on the semolina-dusted sheet pans and leave it uncovered until ready to cook.

To make the pistachio pesto, in a food processor, add the pistachios, mint, garlic, Pecorino Romano, olive oil, salt and freshly ground black pepper, and process until pureed.

Prepare a bowl of ice water. Remove the fava beans from the pod. Blanch the fava beans by cooking them in boiling water until tender, about 1 minute. Remove from the water and place in the ice bath. When cool enough, remove from the water and set aside in a bowl. Remove the waxy outer layer of the bean and discard.

Bring a large pot of salted water to a boil. In the meantime, in a large sauté pan over high heat, add a drizzle of olive oil, garlic, shrimp, crushed red pepper, salt and freshly ground black pepper. While the shrimp are cooking, drop the pasta in the boiling water and cook until al dente, about 3 to 4 minutes. Add the pasta to the sauté pan with white wine and let cook until wine is reduced by half, about a minute.

To serve, divide the pasta between bowls. Garnish with lemon zest and pistachio pesto.

(continued)

GNOCCHETTI WITH FAVA BEANS, SHRIMP AND PISTACHIO PESTO (CONT.)

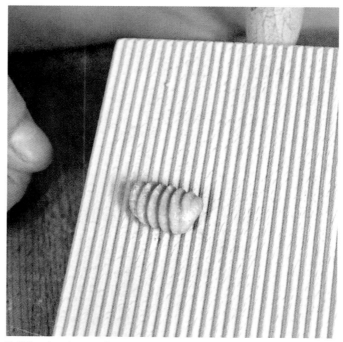

Roll the dough into a rope ½-inch (12-mm) thick and cut into ½-inch (12-mm) pieces. With your thumb gently push dough across board.

Roll the dough away from you to create grooves.

Finished gnocchetti.

CICIONES WITH LENTIL STEW

This is another favorite recipe of mine, due to the aesthetically appealing plating of the dish. The saffron-yellow Sardinian ciciones against the red tomatoes in the dish are fabulous food porn. The balance between the boldness of the saffron and the mild taste of the lentils themselves makes this dish a flavorful little number without beating you over the head with spices.

SERVES 4–6

CICIONES

Semolina Dough (page 21)

6–8 saffron threads

LENTILS

1 cup (200 g) dried lentils

Olive oil

1 onion, diced small

1 carrot, diced small

1 celery stalk, diced small

2 garlic cloves, sliced

¼ cup (59 ml) red wine

1½ cups (355 ml) vegetable stock

1 (28-oz [794-g]) can crushed San Marzano tomatoes

1 bay leaf

Kosher salt

Freshly ground black pepper

TO FINISH

Parmesan, grated

Dust two sheet pans with semolina flour.

To make the ciciones, follow the direction for Semolina Dough, incorporating the saffron with the wet ingredients. Cut off a small piece of dough and cover the rest with plastic wrap. With your hands, roll the piece of dough into a rope about ¼-inch (6-mm) thick. Cut ¼-inch (6-mm) pieces of dough from the rope. Roll the cut pieces between your hands to make chickpea-size balls. Place the ciciones on the semolina-dusted sheet pans and leave it uncovered until ready to cook.

To make the lentils, rinse the lentils with cold water. Heat a large Dutch oven over medium-high heat and add a drizzle of olive oil, onion, carrot, celery and garlic and sauté until soft, about 4 minutes. Add the red wine and let reduce, about 1 minute. Then add the lentils, vegetable stock, San Marzano tomatoes, bay leaf, salt and freshly ground black pepper. Reduce the heat to low and let simmer until the lentils are tender, about 30 to 45 minutes. Remove the bay leaf before serving.

Bring a large pot of salted water to boil. Drop the ciciones in the boiling water and cook until they float, about 1 to 3 minutes. Add the ciciones to the lentils and stir to combine.

To serve, divide the ciciones and lentils between bowls. Garnish with grated Parmesan.

CASARECCE WITH CRISPY ARTICHOKES, LEMON AND SCAMORZA

Literally translated to "homemade," casarecce are the perfect little sauce holders due to their scroll-like shape and texture. I paired the pasta in this recipe with the firm scamorza and crispy artichokes for contrast, and the result is a zesty palate pleaser.

SERVES 4–6

CASARECCE
Semolina Dough (page 21)

CRISPY ARTICHOKES
2 lb (907 g) baby artichokes

Olive oil

Kosher salt

Freshly ground black pepper

TO FINISH
¼ cup (58 g) unsalted butter

Lemon, juice and zest

Scamorza, for grating

Chopped parsley

Preheat the oven to 400°F (204°C) and dust two sheet pans with semolina flour.

To make the casarecce, cut off a small piece of dough and cover the rest of the dough with plastic wrap. With your hands, roll the piece of dough into a rope about ½-inch (12-mm) thick. Cut 2-inch (5-cm) pieces of dough from the rope. Using a wooden skewer, place it in the middle of the dough and press down gently and move your hands in opposite directions. The dough will curl over the skewer and create a twisted look. Carefully remove the skewer and place the casarecce on the semolina dusted sheet pans and leave it uncovered until ready to cook.

Prepare the artichokes by peeling the outer layers until you reach the pale-green inner leaves. Trim about 1 inch (2.5 cm) off the top and then slice the artichokes in half lengthwise. Fill a large bowl with water and squeeze the juice of 1 lemon into the bowl, tossing in the lemon halves as well. Place the cut artichokes into the bowl of lemon water. When all of the artichokes are clean, drain well and place on a sheet pan. Drizzle with olive oil, salt and freshly ground pepper and roast until crispy, about 25 to 30 minutes.

Bring a large pot of salted water to a boil. Meanwhile, in a large sauté pan over medium heat, add the butter, lemon juice and lemon zest. Drop the casarecce in the boiling water and cook until al dente, about 4 to 6 minutes. Add the pasta and artichokes to the pan with the butter and toss to combine. Season with salt and freshly ground black pepper.

To serve, divide the pasta between bowls. Garnish with grated scamorza and chopped parsley.

(continued)

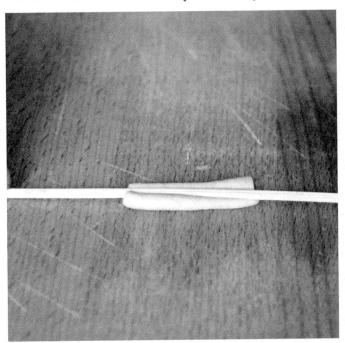

Roll the dough into a rope about ½-inch (12-mm) thick and cut into 2-inch (5-cm) pieces.

Place a skewer in the middle of the dough. Press down gently, moving your hands in opposite directions.

The dough will curl over the skewer and create a twisted pasta.

Finished casarecce.

MEZZI PACCHERI WITH PEAS AND ONIONS

The width of this pasta tube makes it easier to manipulate and shape than some of the more delicate handmade shapes, and also makes it excellent for trapping every bit of sauce. The paccheri are the perfect vessel for the sweet peas and spicy tomato sauce.

SERVES 4–6

MEZZI PACCHERI
Semolina Dough (page 21)

PEAS AND ONIONS
Olive oil

1 onion, diced small

3 garlic cloves, minced

2 cups (302 g) peas

2 (28-oz [794-g]) cans crushed tomatoes

1 tsp crushed red pepper

Kosher salt

Freshly ground black pepper

TO FINISH
Basil, torn

Parmigiano-Reggiano, for grating

Dust two sheet pans with semolina flour.

To make the mezzi paccheri, cut off a small piece of dough and cover the rest with plastic wrap. With your hands, roll the piece of dough into a rope about 1 inch (2.5 cm) thick. Cut 1-inch (2.5-cm) pieces of dough from the rope. Using a rolling pin, roll the cut pieces $\frac{1}{16}$ inch (1.6 mm) thick. Place the handle of a wooden spoon at the edge of the sheet lengthwise and begin rolling the sheet over the handle. Using the palm of your hand to apply pressure, roll back and forth to seal and create a short tube-like shape. Carefully remove the handle and place the paccheri on the semolina-dusted sheet pans and leave it uncovered until ready to cook.

To make the sauce, in a medium-size saucepan over medium heat, add a drizzle of olive oil and sauté the onion and garlic until just translucent, about 3 minutes. Then add the peas, crushed tomatoes and crushed red pepper. Season with salt and freshly ground black pepper. Reduce heat to low and simmer for about 30 minutes.

Bring a large pot of salted water to a boil. Drop the pasta in the water and cook until al dente, about 3 to 4 minutes. Toss the pasta in with the sauce and mix well.

To serve, divide the pasta between bowls. Garnish with freshly torn basil and grated Parmigiano-Reggiano.

(continued)

Place wooden handle at the edge of the dough and begin rolling the dough over handle.

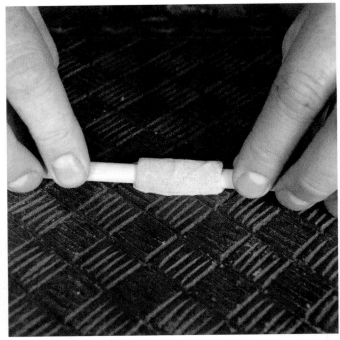

Roll back and forth to seal.

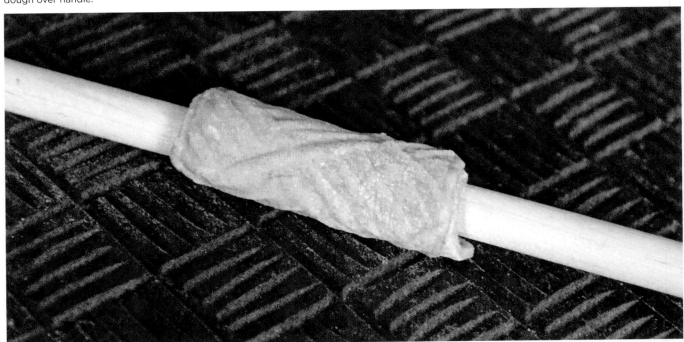

Finished mezzi paccheri.

STROZZAPRETI WITH GREEN TOMATOES AND CRAB

I mostly just threw this one in there because *strozzapreti* translates to "priest-choker" and that is worth mentioning in a handmade pasta book, don't you think? I'm kidding, of course; strozzapreti earned their name by being large enough to choke a person if swallowed whole. I balanced that huge flavor with the lightness of the crab and the tart flavor of the green tomatoes.

SERVES 4-6

STROZZAPRETI
Semolina Dough (page 21)

TO FINISH
8 oz (227 g) green tomatoes

Olive oil

3 garlic cloves, sliced

Crushed red pepper, to taste

8 oz (227 g) crabmeat, picked over

Kosher salt

Freshly ground black pepper

Basil, thinly sliced

1 lemon, zested

Dust two sheet pans with semolina flour.

To make the strozzapreti, divide the dough into four pieces. Place one piece on a lightly floured work surface and cover the rest of the dough with plastic wrap. Begin rolling out the dough until it is about ⅓ inch (8 mm) thick. Using a knife, cut the rolled-out dough into 1½-inch (4-cm) strips. To shape the strozzapreti, pick up one strip and place it in between the palms of your hands. Using a gentle back and forth motion, rub the dough between your hands to create a twisted tube-like shape. Tear off and pinch the rolled dough to create 4-inch (10-cm) pieces. Place the strozzapreti on the semolina-dusted sheet pan and leave it uncovered until ready to cook.

To prepare the green tomatoes, bring a medium-size saucepot of water to boil. Core the tomatoes and use a sharp knife to score the underside of the tomato with an X. Prepare a bowl filled with ice water. Drop the tomatoes in the boiling water and remove after about 30 seconds. Place them in the bowl with ice water. When cool enough to handle, peel and chop the tomatoes.

Bring a large pot of salted water to a boil.

In a large sauté pan over high heat, add a drizzle of olive oil, green tomatoes, garlic and crushed red pepper. Cook for about 2 minutes, tossing frequently. Add the crab and season with salt and pepper. Keep warm.

Drop the strozzapreti in the boiling water and cook until al dente, about 3 to 4 minutes. Add the pasta to the green tomatoes and toss to combine.

To serve, divide the pasta between bowls. Garnish with basil, olive oil and lemon zest.

CHAPTER THREE

GNOCCHI AND GNUDI

Like so many rustic dishes, there are many variations on Italian dumplings. The oldest form—those delightful little nubs we know today as gnocchi—date back to Roman times. Typically made with a semolina-and-egg dough, gnocchi is, in fact, derived from the Italian word nocchio, or "knot in wood." Italian gnocchi varies as much from Italy to Croatia as it does from Abruzzo to Venutto and from table to table. The possibilities and flavor combinations are endless.

Gnudi, on the other hand, are usually described as "nude" ravioli, and are made with cheese and very little flour. They are the light and airy counterpart to their gnocchi cousins and resemble fluffy little pillows.

Whatever your dumpling du jour may be, keep in mind that taste and texture, while they vary from recipe to recipe, are the most important factors in the success of these dumpling dishes. Unlike pasta dough, which is often the structured base for each dish and not necessarily the predominant taste, the flavor of each of the recipes in this chapter lies almost entirely in the dumpling itself.

EGG YOLK GNUDI WITH TRUFFLES

These gnudi are on the lighter side of the dumpling spectrum. The truffle is responsible for the distinctive aroma of the dish, which balances the richness of the egg yolks. If your truffle hog has a head cold and fresh truffles aren't available to you, add some truffle oil at the completion of the recipe. Alternately, you can order truffles online or suss out your local farmers market.

SERVES 4–6

EGG YOLK GNUDI

2 cups (454 g) ricotta cheese

4 egg yolks

1 cup (180 g) grated Parmigiano-Reggiano

Kosher salt

Freshly ground black pepper

½ cup (64 g) 00 flour, plus more for dusting

TRUFFLE BUTTER

½ cup (115 g) unsalted butter

Kosher salt

Freshly ground black pepper

Parmigiano-Reggiano, grated

1 fresh black truffle, shaved

Dust two sheet pans with 00 flour.

To make the gnudi, mix the ricotta cheese, egg yolks, Parmigiano-Reggiano, salt and black pepper in a bowl until well combined. Add the 00 flour and stir until just combined and the mixture comes together. Using two large tablespoons, shape the dough into football shapes and place on the floured sheet pans. Dust with more flour. Make sure the gnudi don't touch or they will stick together. Refrigerate until ready to use.

Bring a large pot of salted water to a boil.

In the meantime, melt the butter in a large sauté pan on medium heat.

Once the water is at a rapid boil, lower the heat down to a simmer and carefully place the egg yolk gnudi in the water and cook for about 1 to 2 minutes or until they float. Using a slotted spoon, add the gnudi to the pan with the melted butter. Season with salt and freshly ground black pepper.

To serve, divide the gnudi between bowls. Garnish with freshly grated Parmigiano-Reggiano and truffle shavings.

PUMPKIN GNOCCHI WITH PANCETTA AND SWISS CHARD PESTO

In many parts of Italy, pumpkin is synonymous with fall flavor. In many parts far and wide, in fact, a pumpkin-spice latte signals the start of scarves-and-Uggs season. I like making this hearty pumpkin gnocchi dish at the first sign of the leaves starting to fall.

SERVES 4–6

PUMPKIN GNOCCHI

½ cup (114 g) ricotta cheese

½ cup (90 g) pumpkin puree

2 eggs

3 cups (381 g) 00 flour, plus more for dusting

½ tsp ground ginger

1 tsp nutmeg, grated

½ tsp ground cloves

1 tbsp (8 g) cinnamon

½ tsp allspice

Kosher salt

Freshly ground black pepper

SWISS CHARD PESTO

Extra-virgin olive oil

8 oz (227 g) Swiss chard, stems removed

½ cup (50 g) grated Pecorino Romano

2 garlic cloves

1 bunch basil

½ cup (63 g) pignoli nuts, toasted

Kosher salt

Freshly ground black pepper

1 cup (237 ml) olive oil

TO FINISH

8 oz (227 g) pancetta, cut into ½-inch (12-mm) pieces

Pecorino Romano

Dust two sheet pans with 00 flour.

To make the gnocchi dough, mix the ricotta cheese, pumpkin puree and eggs in a bowl until well combined. In a separate bowl, mix the 00 flour, ginger, grated nutmeg, cloves, cinnamon, allspice, salt and freshly ground black pepper. Add the flour mixture to the pumpkin-ricotta mixture and stir until just combined and the mixture forms a ball. On a lightly floured surface, lightly knead the dough for about 3 minutes.

To make the gnocchi, cut off a small piece of pumpkin dough and cover the rest with plastic wrap. With your hands, roll the piece of dough into a rope about 1 inch (2.5 cm) wide. Cut 1-inch (2.5-cm) pieces of dough from the rope. Using a gnocchi board or a fork, carefully roll cut gnocchi over the board to form a textured surface. Place the pumpkin gnocchi on the floured sheet pans and make sure the gnocchi don't touch or they will stick together. Refrigerate until ready to use.

To make the Swiss chard pesto, coat a large saute pan with a drizzle of extra-virgin olive oil, add the Swiss chard and cook until wilted. In a food processor, add the wilted chard, Pecorino Romano, garlic, basil, pignoli nuts, salt and freshly ground black pepper. Slowly pour in the olive oil and process until pureed.

Bring a large pot of salted water to a boil.

In the meantime, in a large sauté pan on medium heat, add the pancetta and cook it until the fat is totally rendered out and crispy, about 5 minutes.

Carefully place the gnocchi in the boiling water and cook until they float, about 2 to 3 minutes. Using a slotted spoon, add the pumpkin gnocchi to pancetta pan and toss to combine.

To serve, divide the gnocchi between bowls. Garnish with freshly grated Pecorino Romano and Swiss chard pesto.

SWEET POTATO GNOCCHI WITH PECANS AND PROSCIUTTO

I incorporate sweet potatoes into so many of my standard recipes year-round. Sweet potatoes have a lower glycemic index than other spuds, and they play well with other flavors. I encourage you to make them a regular staple your kitchen as well.

SERVES 4–6

SWEET POTATO GNOCCHI

1 lb (455 g) sweet potatoes, halved lengthwise

Olive oil

Kosher salt

Freshly ground black pepper

1 cup (180 g) grated Parmigiano-Reggiano

1 cup (227 g) ricotta cheese

2 cups (254 g) 00 flour, plus more for dusting

TO FINISH

4 oz (113 g) prosciutto di Parma, thinly sliced

½ cup (115 g) unsalted butter

3 sprigs thyme

Kosher salt

Freshly ground black pepper

Parmigiano-Reggiano

¼ cup (30 g) chopped pecans, toasted

Preheat the oven to 400°F (204°C) and dust two sheet pans with 00 flour.

To make the gnocchi dough, drizzle the potatoes with olive oil and season with salt and freshly ground black pepper. Place on a sheet pan, cut-side down, and roast until fork-tender, about 30 minutes.

Set aside until cool enough to handle. Scoop the flesh out of the skins, then pass the flesh through a potato ricer (or mash with back of a fork) and mix the mashed sweet potato, grated Parmigiano-Reggiano, ricotta cheese, kosher salt and freshly ground black pepper in a bowl until well combined. Add the 00 flour and stir until just combined and the mixture forms a ball. On a lightly floured surface, gently knead the dough for about 3 minutes.

To make the gnocchi, cut off a small piece of sweet potato dough and cover the rest with plastic wrap. With your hands, roll the piece of dough into a rope about 1 inch (2.5 cm) wide. Cut 1-inch (2.5-cm) pieces of dough from the rope. Using a gnocchi board or a fork, carefully roll the cut gnocchi over the board to form a textured surface. Place the sweet potato gnocchi on the floured sheet pans and make sure the gnocchi don't touch or they will stick together. Refrigerate until ready to use.

Place the prosciutto on a parchment-lined sheet pan and bake until crispy, about 6 minutes.

Bring a large pot of salted water to a boil. In the meantime, in a large sauté pan on medium-low heat, add the butter and thyme and cook until brown and has a nutty aroma, about 3 to 4 minutes. Remove sprigs of thyme and discard.

Carefully place the gnocchi in the boiling water and cook until they float, about 2 to 3 minutes. Using a slotted spoon, add the sweet potato gnocchi to the brown butter and toss to combine. Season with salt and freshly ground black pepper. To serve, divide the gnocchi between plates. Garnish with freshly grated Parmigiano-Reggiano, crumbled prosciutto di Parma and chopped pecans.

RAMP GNUDI AND GRANA PADANO

Often the most elbowed-over produce at the farmers market, ramps are a wild leek onion that appears for a very short time at the start of spring. They have a strong, pungent flavor that is a combination of garlic and onion, and the crowd goes absolutely wild for them. They take four years to flower and yield (hence the elbowing). If you can't get your hands on ramps, you can substitute garden-variety leeks and green onions.

SERVES 4–6

RAMP GNUDI

Olive oil

2½ lb (1.1 kg) ramps, chopped

2 cups (454 g) ricotta cheese

2 eggs

1 cup (100 g) grated Grana Padano

Kosher salt

Freshly ground black pepper

½ cup (64 g) 00 flour, plus more for dusting

TO FINISH

½ cup (115 g) unsalted butter

1 bunch thyme

Kosher salt

Freshly ground black pepper

Grana Padano

Dust two sheet pans with 00 flour.

To make the gnudi, in a sauté pan over high heat, add a drizzle of olive oil and chopped ramps. Cook until wilted, about 1 to 2 minutes. In a bowl, mix the wilted ramps, ricotta cheese, eggs, Grana Padano, salt and freshly ground black pepper until well combined. Add the 00 flour and stir until just combined and the mixture forms a ball. Using your hands or a small scoop, shape the mixture into 1-inch (2.5-cm) balls (a little smaller than a golf ball) and place them on the floured sheet pans. Dust with more flour. Make sure the gnudi don't touch or they will stick together. Refrigerate until ready to use.

Bring a large pot of salted water to a boil.

In the meantime, in a large sauté pan, on medium-low heat, add the butter and thyme and cook until brown and has a nutty aroma, about 10 to 12 minutes.

Once the water is at a rapid boil, lower the heat down to a simmer and carefully place the gnudi in the water and cook for about 1 to 2 minutes or until they float. Using a slotted spoon add the ramp gnudi to the pan with brown butter. Season with salt and freshly ground black pepper.

To serve, divide the gnudi between plates. Garnish with freshly grated Grana Padano.

BEET GNOCCHI WITH SHEEP'S MILK RICOTTA AND SAGE

The beets in this gnocchi dish lend a beautiful bright-red color and make it an aesthetically appealing dumpling. They have a very earthy and sweet flavor that pairs well with the simple flavor of the brown butter and sage.

SERVES 4-6

BEET GNOCCHI

1 lb (454 g) red beets, scrubbed and peeled, quartered

Olive oil

Kosher salt

Freshly ground black pepper

2 cups (454 g) sheep's milk ricotta

3 eggs

1 cup (180 g) grated Parmigiano-Reggiano

1 cup (127 g) 00 flour, plus more for dusting

TO FINISH

¼ cup (58 g) unsalted butter

6 sage leaves

Kosher salt

Freshly ground black pepper

Parmigiano-Reggiano

Preheat the oven to 400°F (204°C) and dust two sheet pans with 00 flour.

To make the gnocchi, place beets on a sheet pan and drizzle with olive oil, and season with kosher salt and freshly ground black pepper. Roast until fork-tender, about 45 minutes.

Set aside until cool enough to handle. Pass the beets through a potato ricer (or mash with back of a fork) and mix the beets, sheep's milk ricotta, eggs, Parmigiano-Reggiano, kosher salt and freshly ground black pepper in a bowl until well combined. Add the 00 flour and stir until just combined and the mixture forms a ball.

To make the gnocchi, cut off a small piece of beet dough and cover the rest with plastic wrap. With your hands, roll the piece of dough into a rope about 1 inch (2.5 cm) wide. Cut 1-inch (2.5-cm) pieces of dough from the rope. Using a gnocchi board, carefully roll the cut gnocchi over the board to form a textured surface (or use a fork). Place beet gnocchi on a floured sheet pan and make sure the gnocchi don't touch or they will stick together. Refrigerate until ready to use.

In a large sauté pan, on medium-low heat, add the butter and cook until brown and has a nutty aroma, about 3 to 4 minutes. Add the sage leaves.

Bring a large pot of salted water to a boil.

Once the water is at a rapid boil, lower the heat down a bit and carefully place the gnocchi in the water and cook for about 1 to 2 minutes or until they float. Using a slotted spoon add the beet gnocchi to the pan with brown butter and sage. Season with salt and freshly ground black pepper.

To serve, divide the gnocchi between plates. Garnish with freshly grated Parmigiano-Reggiano.

SAFFRON GNOCCHI WITH BUTTER POACHED LOBSTER AND TARRAGON

I'm just mad about saffron and I'm not alone; saffron was once considered one of the most exotic spices in Renaissance Italy. In this recipe, I exploit the 150 volatile and aroma-yielding compounds in saffron to maximize the flavor of this satisfying lobster dish.

SERVES 4–6

SAFFRON GNOCCHI

2½ lb (1.1 kg) russet potatoes

Olive oil

Kosher salt

Freshly ground black pepper

1 egg

6–8 saffron threads

1 cup (227 g) ricotta cheese

1½ cups (191 g) 00 flour, plus more for dusting

TOMATO SAUCE

Olive oil

1 garlic clove, chopped

1 (28-oz [794-g]) can crushed tomatoes

Crushed red pepper, to taste

BUTTER POACHED LOBSTER

2 (1½-lb [680-g]) lobsters or 3 lobster tails

2 cups (460 g) unsalted butter

2 tbsp (30 ml) vanilla

1 garlic clove, smashed

1 bunch tarragon

TO FINISH

Tarragon, chopped

1 lemon, zested

Preheat the oven to 400°F (204°C) and dust two sheet pans with 00 flour.

To make the gnocchi dough, drizzle the potatoes with olive oil, and season with kosher salt and freshly ground black pepper. Place them on a sheet pan, cut-side down, and roast until fork-tender, about 30 minutes. In a bowl whisk the egg, add the saffron threads and allow to steep for about 3 to 4 minutes. When the potatoes are cool enough to handle, scoop the flesh out of the skins, then pass the flesh through a potato ricer (or mash with back of a fork). Mix the mashed potato, ricotta cheese, egg-saffron mixture, kosher salt and freshly ground black pepper in a bowl until well combined. Add the 00 flour and stir until just combined and the mixture forms a ball. On a lightly floured surface, lightly knead the dough for about 3 minutes.

To make the gnocchi, cut off a small piece of saffron dough and cover the rest with plastic wrap. With your hands, roll the piece of dough into a rope about 1 inch (2.5 cm) wide. Cut 1-inch (2.5-cm) pieces of dough from the rope. Using a gnocchi board, carefully roll the cut gnocchi over the board to form a textured surface (you can also use a fork). Place the saffron gnocchi on a floured sheet pan and make sure the gnocchi don't touch or they will stick together. Refrigerate until ready to use.

To make the sauce, in a saucepan over medium-high heat, add a drizzle of olive oil and garlic and cook for about a minute. Add the can of crushed tomatoes and red pepper flakes. Season to taste with salt and freshly ground black pepper. Allow the sauce to simmer uncovered for about 30 minutes.

(continued)

To make the butter-poached lobster, bring a large pot of water to a boil. Drop the lobster into the pot, cover and let cook for 4 minutes. Remove lobsters and set aside until cool enough to handle. Remove all the lobster meat from the shells and cut into large chunks. In a medium saucepan on low heat, add butter, vanilla, garlic and tarragon. Once the butter is melted, add lobster pieces and allow the lobster to cook for about 5 minutes. Make sure the butter mixture does not come to a boil.

Bring a large pot of salted water to a boil.

In the meantime, in a large sauté pan on low heat, add the butter-poached lobster and some of the tomato sauce.

Carefully place the gnocchi in the boiling water and cook until tender, about 2 to 3 minutes. Using a slotted spoon add the saffron gnocchi to the pan with the lobster and toss to combine. Season with salt and freshly ground black pepper.

To serve, divide the gnocchi and lobster between bowls. Garnish with chopped tarragon and lemon zest.

ROASTED POTATO GNOCCHI WITH ROBIOLA, ARTICHOKES AND CAPERS

This is one of the least labor-intensive recipes in this chapter; potato gnocchi is hearty and resilient, while still producing that "pillow" texture we associate with gnocchi. There is a reason February is National Potato Lover's Month, and this is the glorification of all things potato.

SERVES 4–6

ROASTED POTATO GNOCCHI

2½ lb (1.1 kg) russet potatoes, cut lengthwise

1 bulb garlic

Olive oil

Kosher salt

Freshly ground black pepper

4 sprigs rosemary

2 cups (454 g) ricotta cheese

1 egg

2 cups (254 g) 00 flour, plus more for dusting

½ cup (45 g) chestnut flour

BRAISED ARTICHOKES

2 lemons, one zested

4 medium artichokes

¼ cup (59 ml) olive oil

1 onion, diced

2 garlic cloves, smashed

1 bunch parsley

1 cup (237 ml) white wine

1 cup (237 ml) chicken stock

½ cup (115 g) unsalted butter

ROBIOLA FONDUTA

8 oz (227 g) robiola cheese

¼ cup (59 ml) heavy cream

TO FINISH

¼ cup (60 g) capers, chopped

Italian flat-leaf parsley, chopped

Freshly ground black pepper

Preheat the oven to 400°F (204°C) and dust two sheet pans with 00 flour.

To make the gnocchi dough, drizzle the potatoes and whole bulb of garlic with olive oil, and season with kosher salt and freshly ground black pepper. Place on a sheet pan, cut-side down, with rosemary sprigs, and roast until fork-tender, about 30 minutes. Set aside until cool enough to handle. Scoop the flesh out of the skins, squeeze the garlic out and then pass the flesh through a potato ricer (or mash with back of a fork) and mix the mashed potato, garlic, ricotta cheese, egg, salt and pepper in a bowl until well combined. Add the 00 flour and chestnut flour, stir until just combined and the mixture forms a ball. On a lightly floured surface, gently knead the dough for about 3 minutes.

To make the gnocchi, cut off a small piece of roasted potato dough and cover the rest of the dough with plastic wrap. With your hands, roll the piece of dough into a rope about 1 inch (2.5 cm) wide. Cut 1-inch (2.5-cm) pieces of dough from the rope. Using a gnocchi board, carefully roll the cut gnocchi over the board to form a textured surface (you can use a fork). Place the roasted potato gnocchi on the floured sheet pan and make sure the gnocchi don't touch or they will stick together. Refrigerate until ready to use.

(continued)

ROASTED POTATO GNOCCHI WITH ROBIOLA, ARTICHOKES AND CAPERS (CONT.)

To braise the artichokes, fill a large bowl with water and squeeze the juice of 1 lemon into the bowl, tossing in the lemon halves as well. Rinse each artichoke and trim ½ inch (12 mm) off the stalk. Trim 1 inch (2.5 cm) off the top of each artichoke. Then cut each artichoke in half, from stalk to tip, and remove the choke with a spoon. Remove the tough outer leaves and trim the outside of the stalk with a paring knife. Add the prepared artichokes to the bowl of lemon water to keep them from browning. In a large saucepan over medium heat, add the olive oil, onion, garlic and parsley and cook for about 3 minutes or until the onion is translucent. Add the cleaned artichokes and white wine. Allow for the white wine to reduce by half, about 2 minutes. Add the chicken stock, zest of 1 lemon and butter, cover and cook for about 20 minutes on low heat until tender.

Bring a large pot of salted water to a boil.

To make the fonduta, combine the robiola and heavy cream in a large sauté pan over medium-low heat. Cook, whisking frequently, until the cheese is melted and smooth, about 10 minutes. Reduce the heat to low to keep the sauce warm while the gnocchi cook.

Carefully place the gnocchi in the boiling water and cook until tender, about 2 to 3 minutes. Add the braised artichokes, capers and gnocchi to the robiola sauce and toss to combine.

To serve, divide gnocchi between bowls. Garnish with chopped parsley and freshly ground black pepper.

CRISPY LEMON GNOCCHI WITH SWEET PEAS AND SCALLOPS

Despite the richness of the peas and gnocchi, the lemon and seafood notes make this a perfect summer pasta dish.

SERVES 4–6

LEMON GNOCCHI

1 lb (454 g) russet potatoes

2 eggs

Kosher salt

Freshly ground black pepper

2 Meyer lemons, zested

1¼ cups (210 g) semolina flour, plus more for dusting

¼ cup (10 g) fresh parsley

TO FINISH

1 cup (151 g) fresh peas

½ cup (115 g) unsalted butter

Olive oil

8–12 diver scallops

8 oz (227 g) guanciale, cut into ½-inch (12-mm) pieces

Italian flat-leaf parsley, chopped

1 lemon, zested

Dust two sheet pans with semolina flour. To make the gnocchi dough, in a medium pot, cover the potatoes with cold water. Bring the water to a boil over high heat and cook until the potatoes are fork-tender, about 15 minutes. Drain well and set aside until cool enough to handle. Peel the potatoes and then pass the flesh through a potato ricer (or mash with the back of a fork) and mix the mashed potato, eggs, kosher salt, freshly ground black pepper and lemon zest in a bowl until well combined. Add the semolina flour and chopped parsley and stir until just combined and the mixture forms a ball. On a lightly floured surface, lightly knead the dough for about 3 minutes.

To make the gnocchi, cut off a small piece of lemon dough and cover the rest with plastic wrap. With your hands, roll the piece of dough into a rope about 1-inch (2.5-cm) wide. Cut 1-inch (2.5-cm) pieces of dough from the rope. Place the lemon gnocchi on a semolina-dusted sheet pan. Wrap with plastic wrap and refrigerate until ready to use.

Prepare a bowl of ice water. Blanch the peas by cooking in boiling water until tender, about 1 to 2 minutes. Remove them from the water and place them in an ice bath. When cool enough, remove them from the water and set aside in a bowl.

In a large sauté pan over medium heat, add butter and about 1 tablespoon (15 ml) of olive oil. Working in batches, sauté the gnocchi until golden brown about 3 to 4 minutes on each side. Transfer the crispy lemon gnocchi to a baking sheet.

To sear the scallops, heat a large cast-iron skillet over medium-high heat. Pat scallops dry with a paper towel and sprinkle them evenly with kosher salt and freshly ground black pepper. Add about 1 tablespoon (15 ml) of olive oil and the scallops to the pan; cook 3 minutes on each side or until browned. Remove from pan; keep warm.

To finish, in a large sauté pan, on medium heat, add the guanciale and cook until crispy and the fat is totally rendered out. Add the gnocchi and the peas to the pan with the guanciale. Toss to combine. To serve, divide the gnocchi and scallops between plates. Garnish with fresh parsley and lemon zest.

CHICKPEA GNUDI WITH HEIRLOOM TOMATOES

The high-protein, high-fiber chickpea flour in this recipe makes it a great option for vegetarians. The fresh and springy chickpea base is a lighter alternative to its starchy friend, potato.

SERVES 4–6

CHICKPEA GNUDI

2 cups (454 g) ricotta cheese

1 egg yolk

Kosher salt

Freshly ground black pepper

1½ cups (252 g) semolina flour

1½ cups (138 g) chickpea flour

MARINATED HEIRLOOM TOMATOES

1 lb (454 g) baby heirloom tomatoes, halved

2 garlic cloves, thinly sliced

Basil, torn

¼ cup (59 ml) olive oil

Kosher salt

Freshly ground black pepper

TO FINISH

Pecorino Romano, for grating

Dust two sheet pans with semolina flour.

To make the gnudi, mix the ricotta, egg yolk, salt and freshly ground black pepper in a bowl until well combined. Add the semolina flour and chickpea flour, and stir until just combined and the mixture forms a ball.

Using your hands or a small scoop, shape the mixture into 1-inch (2.5-cm) balls (they should be a little smaller than a golf ball). Place them on the semolina dusted sheet pans. Dust with more semolina. Make sure the gnudi don't touch or they will stick together. Refrigerate until ready to cook.

In a large mixing bowl, add the tomatoes, garlic, basil, olive oil, salt and freshly ground black pepper. Allow it to marinate for about 10 minutes.

Once the water is at a rapid boil, lower the heat to a simmer and carefully place the gnudi in the water and cook for about 1 to 2 minutes or until they float. Using a slotted spoon add the chickpea gnudi to the bowl with the marinated heirloom tomatoes and toss to combine.

To serve, divide the gnudi between plates. Garnish with freshly grated Pecorino Romano.

GNOCCHI VERDI WITH PROVOLONE FONDUTA

These gnocchi are popular in Florence, where the greens grow wild on the hillside. Feel free to use any of your favorite seasonal greens as a substitution for spinach in this recipe.

SERVES 4–6

GNOCCHI

1 lb (455 g) Yukon gold potatoes

Olive oil

¼ lb (113 g) fresh spinach

1¼ cups (210 g) semolina flour, plus more for dusting

1 cup (227 g) ricotta cheese

2 eggs

⅛ tsp freshly grated nutmeg

Kosher salt

Freshly ground black pepper

PROVOLONE FONDUTA

8 oz (227 g) provolone cheese

1 cup (237 ml) heavy cream

Freshly ground black pepper

Dust two sheet pans with semolina flour.

In a medium pot, cover the potatoes with cold water. Bring the water to a boil over high heat and cook until the potatoes are fork-tender, about 15 minutes. Drain well and set aside until cool enough to handle. In the meantime, in a sauté pan, add the olive oil and spinach. Cook until wilted. Peel the potatoes and then pass flesh through a potato ricer (or mash with back of a fork) and mix the mashed potato, wilted spinach, semolina flour, ricotta, eggs, nutmeg, salt and freshly ground black pepper in a bowl until just combined. On a lightly floured surface, lightly knead the dough for about 3 minutes

To make the gnocchi, cut off a small piece of gnocchi dough and cover the rest with plastic wrap. With your hands, roll the piece of dough into a rope about 1 inch (2.5 cm) wide. Cut 1-inch (2.5-cm) pieces of dough from the rope. Using a gnocchi board, carefully roll the cut gnocchi over board to form a textured surface (you can also use a fork). Place the gnocchi on a semolina-dusted sheet pan and make sure the gnocchi don't touch or they will stick together. Refrigerate until ready to use.

To make the sauce, combine the provolone and heavy cream in a large sauté pan over medium-low heat. Cook, whisking frequently, until the cheese is melted and smooth, about 10 minutes. Reduce the heat to low to keep the sauce warm while the gnocchi cook.

Bring a large pot of salted water to a boil. Carefully place the gnocchi in the boiling water and cook until tender, about 2 to 3 minutes.

To serve, divide the gnocchi between bowls. Ladle the fonduta over the top and garnish with freshly ground black pepper.

CHAPTER FOUR

STUFFED PASTA

We have all been told that it's what's inside that counts, and that is certainly the case with the recipes that follow for stuffed pastas. This chapter focuses less on the pasta itself and more on what's inside it. Several of these recipes can be made in large batches or in advance and frozen for dinner another night. Keep in mind, the sky really is the limit with regard to what can be shoved inside these often substantial, sometimes delicate pockets of pasta. I urge you to riff on the variations in these stuffed pasta recipes with what you have on hand in the kitchen, fresh and seasonal ingredients or whatever strikes your fancy.

In terms of technique, stuffed pastas are the best place to experiment with new flavor combinations. Just keep in mind that unlike many of the other chapters in this book, stuffed pastas must maintain their balance. The sheets of pasta, the filling and the sauce in each recipe has to stick to the pasta-to-filling ratio indicated or the dish will fall apart.

POLENTA RAVIOLO WITH GUANCIALE AND WILD MUSHROOMS

Boiled cornmeal, often served as a porridge, is the antiquated association many have with polenta. As in, "Please, sir, can I have some more?" Modern foodies know that polenta is one of the most versatile side dishes around, and I pair it here inside these ravioli with savory guanciale, also known as the magical Roman bacon, for maximum hit-the-spot oomph.

SERVES 4–6

FILLING

1 quart (946 ml) water

1 cup (170 g) cornmeal

¼ cup (58 g) unsalted butter

¼ cup (45 g) grated Parmigiano-Reggiano

1 cup (227 g) ricotta

Kosher salt

Freshly ground black pepper

6–12 egg yolks

RAVIOLO

Ravioli Dough (page 20)

TO FINISH

4 oz (113 g) guanciale, cut into ½-inch (12-mm) pieces

Olive oil

1 lb (454 g) wild mushrooms

3 sprigs thyme

Kosher salt

Freshly ground black pepper

Parmigiano-Reggiano, for grating

To make the filling bring 4 cups (946 ml) of water to a boil. Slowly whisk in the cornmeal and reduce the heat to low. Cook, stirring frequently, until the mixture thickens and is tender, about 15 minutes. Add the butter and Parmigiano-Reggiano. Allow the mixture to cool and then add the ricotta, salt and freshly ground black pepper and mix well.

Dust two sheet pans with semolina flour.

To make the pasta, roll out the dough until the sheets are just translucent (see page 17). Cut the rolled out sheets into 12-inch (30-cm) sections and cover the rest with plastic wrap. Lay the sheets on a dry work surface, and starting at one end of the sheet, using a piping bag or a spoon, spread about 3 tablespoons (45 g) of filling down the entire length of the pasta sheet, leaving about 1 inch (2.5 cm) between each dollop. Then, with your fingers, create a nest in the filling. Carefully place an egg yolk in each nest and cover the filling with another sheet of pasta over the top. Use a spritz of water to help seal it if necessary. As you drape the pasta over the filling, carefully press down to seal and make sure there is no air trapped inside. Using a round 3-inch (7.5-cm) cutter, punch out the raviolo and carefully place on the semolina-dusted sheet pan, spaced apart.

Bring a large pot of salted water to a boil.

In a large sauté pan over medium heat, add the guanciale and cook until crispy and the fat is rendered out, about 5 minutes. Keep warm. In another sauté pan, on medium heat add a drizzle of olive oil, mushrooms, thyme, salt and freshly ground pepper and cook until tender, about 6 minutes.

Carefully drop the pasta in the boiling water and cook until they are al dente, about 2 minutes. Add the pasta to the pan with the guanciale and carefully shake the pan so the pasta becomes coated with the guanciale fat.

To serve, divide the pasta between plates. Garnish with mushrooms and freshly grated Parmigiano-Reggiano.

EGGPLANT MEZZALUNA WITH TOMATO CONFIT AND PESTO

Half-moon ravioli is a staple, but my twist is I pair it with slow-roasted tomato confit, which acts as both a condiment complement to the pesto sauce and as an airy balance to the hearty eggplant.

SERVES 4-6

FILLING

Olive oil

2 eggplants, peeled and diced

3 garlic cloves, minced

1 onion, diced

Kosher salt

Freshly ground black pepper

¼ cup (45 g) Parmigiano-Reggiano

1 cup (130 g) grated mozzarella

TOMATO CONFIT

4 plum tomatoes

Olive oil

3 sprigs rosemary

3 sprigs thyme

1 garlic clove, thinly sliced

½ tsp sugar

Kosher salt

Freshly ground black pepper

MEZZALUNA

Ravioli Dough (page 20)

PESTO

2 cups (50 g) basil

½ cup (90 g) grated Parmigiano-Reggiano

2 garlic cloves

¼ cup (32 g) pignoli nuts

Kosher salt

Freshly ground black pepper

⅔ cup (160 ml) olive oil

Preheat oven to 325°F (163°C).

In a large sauté pan, over medium-high heat, add a drizzle of olive oil, eggplant, garlic, onion, salt and freshly ground black pepper. Cook until the eggplant is soft, about 8 minutes. Remove from the heat and allow it to cool. In a bowl mix the cooked eggplant, Parmigiano-Reggiano and mozzarella.

To make the tomato confit, cut the tomatoes in half lengthwise and scoop out the seeds. On a sheet pan, drizzle some olive oil and place the tomatoes cut-side down with the rosemary, thyme and garlic. Season with sugar, salt and freshly ground black pepper. Bake until they are shriveled and dark red, about 45 minutes.

Dust two sheet pans with semolina flour. To make the pasta, roll out the dough until the sheet is just translucent (see page 17). Cut the rolled-out sheets into 12-inch (30-cm) sections and cover the rest with plastic wrap. Lay the sheets on a dry work surface and using a round 3-inch (7.5-cm) cutter, cut circles into the sheet. Using a piping bag or a spoon, place filling in the middle of the pasta circle, leaving about ¼ inch (6 mm) around the sides. To seal, fold the circle over to create a half-moon shape and use a fork to press along the edges to seal. Use a spritz of water to help seal it if necessary. Carefully place the mezzaluna on the semolina-dusted sheet pans, spaced apart.

To make the pesto, in a food processor, add basil, grated Parmigiano-Reggiano, garlic, pignoli nuts, kosher salt and freshly ground black pepper. Slowly pour in the olive oil and process until pureed.

Bring a large pot of salted water to a boil. Carefully drop the pasta in the boiling water and cook until al dente, about 2 to 3 minutes.

In a sauté pan over low heat, add a drizzle of olive oil and the tomato confit. Add the pasta to the pan and gently shake the pan to mix with the tomatoes. Season with salt and freshly ground black pepper. To serve, divide the pasta between plates. Garnish with pesto.

(continued)

EGGPLANT MEZZALUNA WITH TOMATO CONFIT
AND PESTO (CONT.)

Place the filling in the middle of the pasta circle.

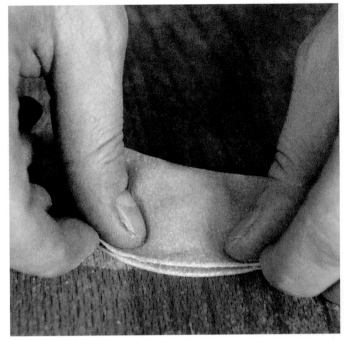

Fold the circle to create a half-moon shape.

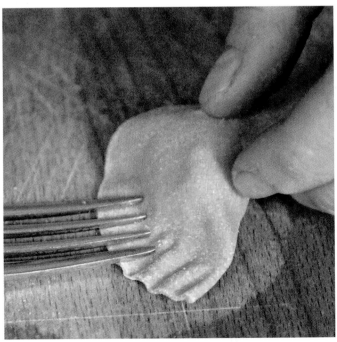

Using a fork, press down along the edges to seal.

Finished mezzaluna.

BUTTERNUT SQUASH AND ROASTED PEAR CAPPELLACCI WITH SAGE

Cappellacci, from the Ferrara region, is often stuffed with some sort of gourd, and this recipe is no exception. I use butternut squash, a fall staple in any Italian kitchen, with complementary sweet and savory notes.

SERVES 4–6

FILLING

1 butternut squash, halved lengthwise, seeds removed

Olive oil

Kosher salt

Freshly ground black pepper

3 Bosc pears, peeled, cored and sliced

¼ tsp grated nutmeg

½ cup (90 g) grated Parmigiano-Reggiano

1 egg

CAPPELLACCI

Ravioli Dough (page 20)

TO FINISH

¼ cup (58 g) unsalted butter

1 bunch sage

Kosher salt

Freshly ground black pepper

Parmigiano-Reggiano, for grating

Preheat the oven to 375°F (190°C).

To make the filling, place the cut butternut squash on a sheet pan and drizzle the cut side with olive oil. Season with salt and pepper. Cook for about 45 minutes or until fork-tender. While cooling the butternut squash, drizzle the pears with olive oil and cook until soft, about 10 to 15 minutes. Scoop out the squash flesh and place in a food processor with the pears, olive oil, nutmeg, Parmigiano-Reggiano and egg; pulse until smooth. Season with salt and freshly ground pepper.

Dust two sheet pans with semolina flour.

To make the pasta, roll out the dough until the sheet is just translucent (see page 17). Cut the rolled out sheets into 12-inch (30-cm) sections and cover the rest with plastic wrap. Lay the sheets on a dry work surface and, using a straight wheel cutter or a knife, cut the pasta sheets into 2-inch (5-cm) squares. Using a piping bag or a spoon, place about 1 tablespoon (15 g) of filling in the middle of each square, leaving about ¼ inch (6 mm) around the sides. To seal, fold the square over to the opposite corner to form a triangle shape and use your fingers to press along the edges to seal. Take the two opposite ends of the triangle and pinch them together. Use a spritz of water to help seal it if necessary. Carefully place the cappellacci on the semolina-dusted sheet pans, spaced apart.

Bring a large pot of salted water to a boil. Carefully drop the pasta in the water and cook until al dente, about 2 to 3 minutes.

To finish, in a large sauté pan over medium-low heat, add the butter and sage, and cook until the butter is brown and it has a nutty aroma, about 3 to 4 minutes. Add the pasta to the pan and toss to combine. Season with salt and freshly ground black pepper.

To serve, divide the pasta between plates. Garnish with some grated Parmigiano-Reggiano.

(continued)

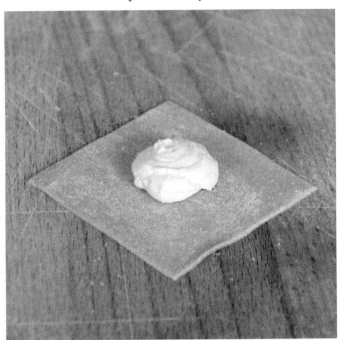

Place the filling in the middle of the square.

Fold the square over to the opposite corner, forming a triangle shape.

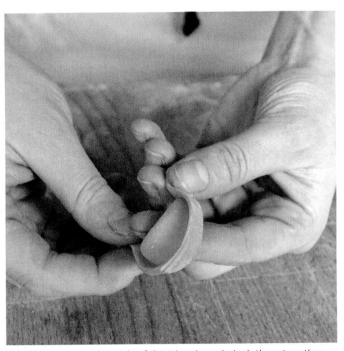

Take the two opposite ends of the triangle and pinch them together to seal.

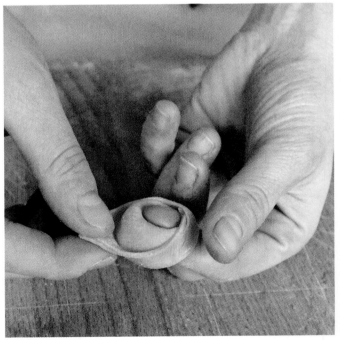

Finished cappellacci.

VEAL AGNOLOTTI WITH MUSTARD GREENS AND PECORINO

Hailing from the Piedmont region, agnolotti features delicate layers of flattened dough. Combined with the tender veal, it creates a light dish with a spicy kick from the mustard greens.

SERVES 4–6

FILLING

Olive oil

1 lb (454 g) ground veal

3 garlic cloves, chopped

1 lb (454 g) mustard greens, chopped

1 tsp freshly grated nutmeg

1 bunch Italian flat-leaf parsley, chopped

Kosher salt

Freshly ground black pepper

½ cup (50 g) grated Pecorino Romano

AGNOLOTTI

Ravioli Dough (page 20)

TO FINISH

¼ cup (58 g) unsalted butter

Pecorino Romano, for grating

Baby mustard greens

To make the filling, in a sauté pan on medium-high medium heat, add a drizzle of olive oil and veal. Cook until brown, about 8 to 10 minutes. Drain off the excess grease and set aside. In a sauté pan on medium heat, add a drizzle of olive oil, garlic, mustard greens, nutmeg and parsley. Cook until the parsley is wilted, about 2 to 3 minutes. Season with salt and freshly ground pepper. Add the greens to the cooked veal. Stir in grated Pecorino Romano. Place the veal-and-mustard-greens mixture in a food processor and pulse until it comes together.

Dust two sheet pans with semolina flour.

To make the pasta, roll out the dough until the sheet is just translucent (see page 17). Cut the rolled-out sheets into 12-inch (30-cm) sections and cover the rest with plastic wrap. Lay the sheets on a dry work surface and, using a straight wheel cutter or a knife, cut the pasta sheets lengthwise into two 3-inch (7.5-cm-) wide strips. Using a piping bag or a spoon, place the filling down the middle of each sheet in a row. To seal, fold the pasta over the filling to the opposite side, leaving about ¼ inch (6 mm) of dough bare. Use a spritz of water to help seal it if necessary. To form the individual agnolotti, pinch the dough with your thumb and index finger. Work your way down the entire length of the sheet, individually sealing and pinching to create 2-inch (5-cm) pastas. Using a fluted pasta wheel, trim the edge of the dough along the entire length, getting as close to the filling as possible. To cut the pasta into individual agnolotti, using a fluted cutter, quickly and with force, cut them directly in the middle of the pinch. Carefully place the agnolotti on the semolina-dusted sheet pans, spaced apart.

Bring a large pot salted of water to boil. Carefully drop the pasta in the water and cook until al dente, about 2 to 3 minutes. Meanwhile, in a large sauté pan over medium heat, add the butter and melt. Then add the cooked pasta and toss to combine.

To serve, divide the pasta between plates. Garnish with grated Pecorino Romano and some baby mustard greens.

(continued)

Place the filling down the entire length of the dough.

Fold the pasta over the filling and press down to seal.

Pinch the dough with your thumb and index finger every 2 inches (5 cm).

Using a pastry wheel, trim the edge of the dough as close to the filling as possible.

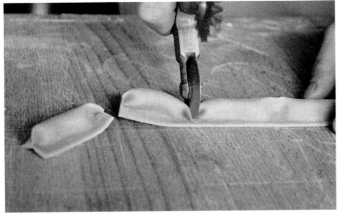

Then cut directly in the middle of the "pinch."

Finished agnolotti.

PROSCIUTTO CARAMELLE WITH GORGONZOLA FONDUTA

Not to be confused with the candy preparation of the same name, this pasta is traditionally served in Parma at brunch time or as a holiday teaser before the main course. The rich Gorgonzola and salty prosciutto come together in this pasta to create a very unique flavor profile.

SERVES 4–6

FILLING
Olive oil

1 lb (454 g) prosciutto, diced small

1 head radicchio, chopped

2 cups (454 g) ricotta

Kosher salt

Freshly ground black pepper

CARAMELLE
Ravioli Dough (page 20)

GORGONZOLA FONDUTA
8 oz (227 g) Gorgonzola

¼ cup (59 ml) heavy cream

TO FINISH
Freshly ground black pepper

1 lemon, zested

To make the filling, in a large sauté pan over high heat, add a drizzle of olive oil and prosciutto and cook until crispy, about 3 to 4 minutes. Then add radicchio and cook until wilted, about 2 minutes. Remove from heat. In a bowl, combine the prosciutto, radicchio and ricotta, and season with salt and freshly ground black pepper.

Dust two sheet pans with semolina flour.

To make the pasta, roll out the dough until the sheet is just translucent (see page 17). Cut the rolled-out sheets into 12-inch (30-cm) sections and cover the rest with plastic wrap. Lay the sheets on a dry work surface and, using a straight wheel cutter or a knife, cut the pasta sheets into rectangles 3 inches (7.5 cm) long by 2 inches (5 cm) wide. Using a piping bag or a spoon, place 2-inch (5-cm) logs of filling down the length of the rectangle close to the edge, leaving about ½ inch (12 mm) of space on each side. To seal, fold the bottom edge over the filling and carefully roll the pasta away from you to form a tube-like shape. Use a spritz of water to help seal it if necessary. Pinch down the sides, sealing the dough where the filling ends and using your thumbs to pinch both ends, and twist about 180 degrees and pinch again. Carefully place the caramelle on the semolina-dusted sheet pans, spaced apart.

Bring a large pot of salted water to a boil. Carefully drop the pasta in the water and cook until al dente, about 2 to 3 minutes.

To make the fonduta, combine the gorgonzola and heavy cream in a large sauté pan over medium-low heat. Cook, whisking frequently, until the cheese is melted and smooth, about 10 minutes. Reduce the heat to low and keep warm while the pasta cooks. Then add the cooked pasta and toss to combine.

To serve, divide the pasta between bowls. Garnish with freshly ground black pepper and lemon zest.

(continued)

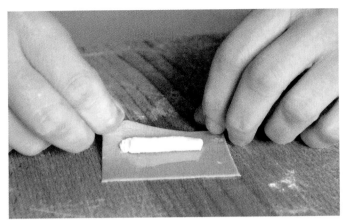

Place the filling down the length of the rectangle close to the edge.

Fold the bottom edge over the filling.

Carefully roll the pasta away from you, creating a tube-like shape.

Press down on both ends of the dough to seal.

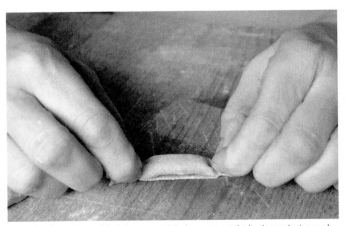

Pinch both ends and twist about 180 degrees and pinch again to seal.

Finished caramelle.

ANOLINI IN BRODO

Traditionally served in broth over the holiday season, this stuffed pasta from Parma is an excellent choice for a winter night or any time comfort food is called for. The meat filling is a nice alternative to a winter stew, without the weight and heft, even though it is made with similar ingredients. Same satisfied feeling, less chance of a food coma.

SERVES 4–6

FILLING

¼ cup (58 g) unsalted butter

1 garlic clove, chopped

1 lb (454 g) ground beef

Kosher salt

Freshly ground black pepper

½ cup (60 g) bread crumbs

½ cup (90 g) Parmigiano-Reggiano

BRODO

Olive oil

2 garlic cloves, chopped

2 celery stalks, diced small

2 carrots, diced small

1 onion, diced small

1 bunch parsley, chopped

Kosher salt

Freshly ground black pepper

ANOLINI

Ravioli Dough (page 20)

TO FINISH

Parmigiano-Reggiano, for grating

Italian flat-leaf parsley, chopped

Dust two sheet pans with semolina flour.

To make the filling, in a large sauté pan over medium-high heat melt the butter. Add the garlic and ground beef. Cook until done, about 5 to 8 minutes. Drain off the excess grease and season with salt and freshly ground black pepper. Once slightly cooled, pulse in food processor with the bread crumbs and Parmigiano-Reggiano until combined.

To make the brodo, in a large saucepot over high heat, add a drizzle of olive oil, garlic, celery, carrots, onion and parsley. Cover with about 1½ quarts (1.4 L) of water and bring to a boil. Then reduce to medium-low and simmer for about 45 minute. Season with salt and freshly ground black pepper.

To make the pasta, roll out the dough until the sheet is just translucent (see page 17). Cut the rolled-out sheets into 12-inch (30-cm) sections and cover the rest with plastic wrap. Lay the sheets on a dry work surface, and starting at one end of the sheet, use a piping bag or a spoon to place about ½ teaspoon of filling down the entire length of the pasta sheet in two rows, leaving about ½ inch (12 mm) between each dollop. Cover the filling with another sheet of pasta over the top. Use a spritz of water to help seal it if necessary. As you drape the pasta over the filling, carefully press down to seal and make sure there is no air trapped inside. Using a round 1-inch (2.5-cm) cutter, punch out the anolini and carefully place them on the semolina-dusted sheet pans, spaced apart.

Bring the brodo back to a boil and carefully drop the pasta in and cook until al dente, about 2 to 3 minutes.

To serve, divide the pasta between bowls with brodo. Garnish with Parmigiano-Reggiano and chopped parsley.

SWEET PEA RAVIOLINI WITH MASCARPONE AND MINT

This seasonal vegetable pasta works as a first course or as the main attraction; the unique peppery flavor of the watercress dominates this otherwise delicate pasta, elevating it beyond your average raviolini dish.

SERVES 4–6

FILLING

Olive oil

4 cups (604 g) peas

Kosher salt

Freshly ground black pepper

1 bunch mint

1½ cups (341 g) mascarpone

½ cup (90 g) grated Parmigiano-Reggiano

1 lemon, juice and zest

RAVIOLINI

Ravioli Dough (page 20)

TO FINISH

8 oz (227 g) watercress

1 lemon, juice and zest

Kosher salt

Freshly ground black pepper

¼ cup (58 g) unsalted butter

Olive oil

Dust two sheet pans with semolina flour.

To make the filling, in a large sauté pan over medium high heat, drizzle olive oil. Add the peas and cook until bright green, about 2 to 5 minutes. Season with salt and freshly ground black pepper. Pulse the cooked peas, mint leaves, mascarpone, Parmigiano-Reggiano and lemon juice in a food processor until it comes together. Reserve about ¼ cup (60 g) of filling to make a sauce.

To make the pasta, roll out the dough until the sheet is just translucent (see page 17). Cut the rolled out sheets into 12-inch (30-cm) sections and cover the rest with plastic wrap. Lay the sheets on a dry work surface and starting at one end of the sheet, use a piping bag or a spoon to place about 2 teaspoons (10 g) of filling down the entire length of the pasta sheet in two rows, leaving about 1 inch (2.5 cm) between each dollop. Use a spritz of water to help seal it if necessary. As you drape the pasta over the filling, carefully press down to seal and make sure there is no air trapped inside. Using a 2-inch (5-cm) ravioli stamp or a pasta wheel, cut 2-inch (5-cm) squares or circles and carefully place the raviolini on the semolina-dusted sheet pans, spaced apart.

Bring a large pot of salted water to a boil. Carefully drop the pasta in the water and cook until al dente, about 2 to 3 minutes. In a large sauté pan, over medium heat, add butter and melt. Then add the cooked pasta to the pan with reserved filling and toss to combine.

To finish, divide the pasta between plates. In a small bowl, combine the watercress with a drizzle of olive oil, lemon juice, salt and freshly ground black pepper. Garnish the pasta with the dressed watercress.

ESPRESSO BRAISED SHORT RIB AND CELERY ROOT RAVIOLI

In an attempt to incorporate all the things I like in one pasta, I found the perfect combination. The idea of adding espresso may seem innovative, but the method of enhancing sauces with coffee and espresso is as old as the art of cultivating the beans themselves.

SERVES 4–6

BRAISED SHORT RIBS

3 lb (1.4 kg) short ribs

Kosher salt

Freshly ground black pepper

Olive oil

2 carrots, diced

2 celery stalks, diced

2 onions, diced

3 garlic cloves, chopped

1 cup (237 ml) red wine

4 sprigs thyme

1 bunch parsley

4 sprigs rosemary

1 bay leaf

3 tbsp (10 g) instant espresso

1 qt (946 ml) beef stock

CELERY ROOT PUREE

1 large celery root

3 tbsp (43 g) unsalted butter

½ cup (119 ml) heavy cream

1 bay leaf

Kosher salt

Freshly ground black pepper

RAVIOLI

Ravioli Dough (page 20)

TO FINISH

¼ cup (58 g) unsalted butter

Chives, thinly sliced

Preheat the oven to 375°F (190°C). Generously season the ribs with salt and pepper. Heat a Dutch oven over high heat and add a drizzle of olive oil. Working in batches, add the short ribs and sear on all sides, until a nice brown crust forms. Remove and set aside. In the same Dutch oven, add a drizzle of olive oil, carrots, celery, onions and garlic. Cook until they are soft and have color, about 3 to 4 minutes. Add red wine to deglaze the pan, using a spoon to scrape up all of the bits at the bottom. Return the short ribs to the pan and then add the thyme, parsley, rosemary, bay leaf, espresso, salt, freshly ground black pepper and enough beef stock to cover the short ribs. Cover the pot and place in the oven. Cook for about 4 hours or until the meat is fork-tender. Remove the bay leaf before serving.

To make the celery root puree, peel the celery root and cut into medium-size pieces. In a medium saucepan over low heat, add the butter and cut celery root. Cook until soft, about 6 minutes. Add the heavy cream and bay leaf and allow to simmer for about 2 minutes. Remove the bay leaf. Add the celery root and heavy cream to a food processor and process until smooth. Season with salt and pepper.

Dust two sheet pans with semolina flour. To make the pasta, roll out the dough until the sheet is just translucent (see page 17). Cut the rolled-out sheets into 12-inch (30-cm) sections and cover the rest with plastic wrap. Lay the sheets on a dry work surface and, starting at one end of the sheet, use a piping bag or a spoon to place about 2 tablespoons (30 g) of celery root puree down the entire length of the pasta sheet in two rows, leaving about 1 inch (2.5 cm) between each dollop. Place about 1 tablespoon (15 g) of braised short rib on top of the celery root. As you drape the pasta over the filling, carefully press down to seal and make sure there is no air trapped inside. Use a spritz of water to help seal it if necessary. Using a 4-inch (10-cm) ravioli stamp or a pasta wheel, cut 4-inch (10-cm) squares or circles and carefully place the ravioli on the semolina-dusted sheet pans, spaced apart.

Bring a large pot of salted water to a boil. Meanwhile in a small sauté pan on medium-high heat, melt the butter. To serve, divide the pasta between bowls. Garnish with melted butter and chives.

RADICCHIO AND TALEGGIO TRIANGOLI WITH PORK CHEEK RAGU

The shape of the triangoli in this recipe allows for the perfect amount of filling per bite in this dish. Pork cheeks are one of those "specialty cuts" most people are very hesitant about. They are also one of the most underrated and best cuts for braising because they have just the right amount of fat. The meat almost melts in your mouth and is perfect when paired with the bitter radicchio.

SERVES 4–6

PORK CHEEK RAGU

3 lb (1.4 kg) pork cheek

Kosher salt

Freshly ground black pepper

Olive oil

2 carrots, diced

1 celery stalk, diced

1 onion, diced

3 garlic cloves, chopped

1 (6-oz [170-g]) can tomato paste

½ cup (118 ml) red wine

1 bunch Italian flat-leaf parsley

3 sprigs rosemary

4 sprigs thyme

1 bay leaf

1 (28-oz [794-g]) can crushed tomatoes

3 cups (711 ml) beef stock

FILLING

Olive oil

1 head radicchio, thinly sliced

1 lb (454 g) Taleggio, grated

1 lemon, zest and juice

TRIANGOLI

Ravioli Dough (page 20)

TO FINISH

Italian flat-leaf parsley, chopped

Preheat the oven to 375°F (190°C).

To make the pork cheek ragu, generously season the pork with salt and freshly ground black pepper. To a Dutch oven over high heat, add a drizzle of olive oil. Working in batches, add the pork cheeks and sear on all sides, until a nice brown crust forms. Remove and set aside. In the same Dutch oven, add a drizzle of olive oil, carrots, celery, onion and garlic. Cook until they are soft and golden, about 3 to 4 minutes. Add the tomato paste and stir constantly to avoid burning. Then add red wine to deglaze the pan, and use a spoon to scrape up all of the bits at the bottom. Return the pork cheek to the pan and then add the parsley, rosemary, thyme, bay leaf, salt, freshly ground black pepper, crushed tomatoes and enough beef stock to cover the pork. Cover the pot and place in the oven. Cook for about 4 hours or until the meat is fork-tender. When cool enough to handle, break the meat apart with two forks and remove the bay leaf. Keep warm.

To make the filling, in a medium-size sauté pan, add a drizzle of olive oil and the radicchio. Cook until wilted, about 3 minutes. Allow to cool. In a large mixing bowl, combine wilted radicchio, Taleggio, lemon zest and lemon juice. Season with salt and freshly ground black pepper.

Dust two sheet pans with semolina flour.

(continued)

RADICCHIO AND TALEGGIO TRIANGOLI WITH PORK CHEEK RAGU (CONT.)

To make the pasta, roll out the dough until the sheet is just translucent (see page 17). Cut the rolled-out sheets into 12-inch (30-cm) sections and cover the rest with plastic wrap. Lay the sheets on a dry work surface and, using a straight wheel cutter or a knife, cut the pasta sheets into 3-inch (7.5-cm) squares. Using a piping bag or a spoon, place about 1 teaspoon of filling in the middle, leaving about ¼ inch (6 mm) of dough bare on the edge. To seal, fold the square over to the opposite corner to form a triangle shape and use your fingers to press along the edges to seal. Use a spritz of water to help seal it if necessary. With a fluted cutter, trim along the edges, leaving about ¼ inch (6 mm) of pasta around the filling. Carefully place the triangoli on the semolina-dusted sheet pans, spaced apart.

Bring a large pot of salted water to a boil. Carefully drop the pasta in the water and cook until al dente, about 2 to 3 minutes.

In a large sauté pan over medium heat, add some pork ragu and the cooked pasta. Toss to combine.

To serve, divide the pasta between bowls. Garnish with chopped parsley.

Place the filling in the middle of the pasta square.

Fold the square over to the opposite corner to form a triangle shape.

Press down along the edges to seal. Using a fluted cutter, trim along the edges.

Finished triangoli.

SUNCHOKE CAPPELLETTI WITH KALE AND APPLES

These "little hats" are traditionally served in a broth most famously in the Gubbio region on Christmas. In a twist on a classic, I infused some summer produce into the mix for a lighter dinner option.

SERVES 4–6

FILLING

Olive oil

4 lb (1.8 kg) sunchokes, chopped

2 garlic cloves, chopped

1 cup (227 g) ricotta

Kosher salt

Freshly ground black pepper

CAPPELLETTI

Ravioli Dough (page 20)

TO FINISH

Olive oil

1 lb (454 g) kale, chopped

1 apple, thinly sliced

To make the filling, in a large sauté pan on medium-high heat, drizzle olive oil and add the sunchokes. Cook until soft, about 8 to 10 minutes. Remove from the heat and let cool slightly. In a food processor, pulse the sunchokes, garlic and ricotta until combined. Season with salt and freshly ground black pepper.

Dust two sheet pans with semolina flour.

To make the pasta, roll out the dough until the sheet is just translucent (see page 17). Cut the rolled-out sheets into 12-inch (30-cm) sections and cover the rest with plastic wrap. Lay the sheets on a dry work surface and, using a round 3-inch (7.5-cm) cutter, cut circles into the sheets. Using a piping bag or a spoon, place about 1 teaspoon of filling in the middle of the pasta circle, leaving about ¼ inch (6 mm) around the sides. Fold the circle over to create a half-moon shape and press along the edges to seal. Use a spritz of water to help seal it if necessary. To form the pasta shape, with the curved edge facing you, bring the two points together and press. Gently make sure the curved outer edge is up to form a circular shape. Set the pasta on your work surface, making sure that it stands on its own. Carefully transfer the cappelletti to the semolina-dusted sheet pans, spaced apart.

Bring a large pot of water to a boil. Meanwhile, in a large sauté pan, on medium heat, drizzle olive oil. Add the kale and sauté until it starts to wilt. Turn off the heat and toss in the apples. Season with salt and freshly ground pepper.

Carefully drop the pasta in the water and cook until al dente, about 2 to 3 minutes. Toss in the sauté pan with the kale and apples.

To serve, divide the pasta, kale and apples between bowls.

FAGGOTINI WITH DILL, SHRIMP AND ZUCCHINI

These "little bundles" of faggotini hold a light and airy summer assortment of shrimp and zucchini; feel free to throw in other seasonal vegetables to taste.

SERVES 4–6

FILLING

Olive oil

1 zucchini, diced small

1 lb (454 g) shrimp, chopped

1 lemon, juice and zest

1 bunch parsley, chopped

1 cup (227 g) ricotta cheese

½ cup (90 g) Parmigiano-Reggiano

Kosher salt

Freshly ground black pepper

FAGGOTINI

Ravioli Dough (page 20)

1 bunch dill, chopped

TO FINISH

Dill fronds, picked

To make the filling, in a large sauté pan on medium-high heat drizzle the olive oil. Sauté the zucchini until soft, about 5 to 8 minutes. Set aside. Drizzle more olive oil and sauté the shrimp until cooked through, about 5 to 8 minutes. In a medium bowl, mix the chopped shrimp, zucchini, lemon, parsley, ricotta and Parmigiano-Reggiano until well combined. Season with salt and freshly ground black pepper.

Dust two sheet pans with semolina flour.

To make the dill dough, follow the instructions for Ravioli Dough, incorporating the chopped dill with the wet ingredients.

To make the pasta, roll out the dough until the sheet is just translucent (see page 17). Cut the rolled-out sheets into 12-inch (30-cm) sections and cover the rest with plastic wrap. Lay the sheets on a dry work surface and, using a straight wheel cutter or a knife, cut the dough into 3-inch (7.5-cm) squares. Using a piping bag or a spoon, place about 1 tablespoon (15 g) of filling in the middle of the square, leaving about ½ inch (12 mm) around the sides. Bring the four corners together to form a bundle. Pinch and twist at the top to seal. Use a spritz of water to help seal it if necessary. Carefully place the faggotini on the semolina-dusted sheet pans, spaced apart.

Bring a large pot of water to a boil. Carefully drop the pasta in the water and cook until al dente, about 2 to 3 minutes.

To serve, divide the pasta between bowls. Garnish with dill fronds.

ARTICHOKE CASONSEI WITH HAZELNUTS AND GOAT'S MILK RICOTTA

These sheets of pasta wrapped around a light artichoke filling hail from the Lombardy region and are an excellent vegetarian pasta choice. The hazelnuts add a nice crunch and layer of flavor to this dish.

SERVES 4–6

FILLING

2 lb (907 g) artichokes

2 lemons

¼ cup (59 ml) olive oil

1 onion, diced

2 garlic cloves, smashed

1 bunch Italian flat-leaf parsley

1 cup (237 ml) white wine

1 cup (237 ml) chicken stock

½ cup (115 g) unsalted butter

2 cups (454 g) goat's milk ricotta

CASONSEI

Ravioli Dough (page 20)

TO FINISH

Italian flat-leaf parsley, chopped

½ cup (86 g) hazelnuts, chopped

To braise the artichokes, fill a large bowl with water and the juice of 1 lemon; toss in the lemon halves as well. Rinse each artichoke and trim ½ inch (12 mm) off the stalk. Trim 1 inch (2.5 cm) off the top of each artichoke. Then cut the artichoke in half, from the stalk to the tip, and remove the choke with a spoon. Remove the tough outer leaves and trim the outside of the stalk with a paring knife. Add the prepared artichokes to the bowl of lemon water to keep them from browning. In a large saucepot over medium heat, add the olive oil, onion, garlic and parsley, and cook for about 3 minutes or until translucent. Add the cleaned artichokes and white wine. Allow the white wine to reduce by half, about 2 minutes. Add the chicken stock, zest of one lemon and butter, cover and cook for about 20 minutes on low heat until tender. To make the filling, pulse the braised artichokes in a food processor with the ricotta until combined.

Dust two sheet pans with semolina flour. To make the pasta, roll out the dough until the sheet is just translucent (see page 17). Cut the rolled out sheets into 12-inch (30-cm) sections and cover the rest with plastic wrap. Lay the sheets on a dry work surface and, using a straight wheel cutter or a knife, cut the pasta sheets lengthwise into two 3-inch (7.5-cm) wide strips. Using a piping bag or a spoon, place 1½-inch (3.8-cm) logs of filling down the middle of each sheet in a row, leaving about 1 inch (2.5 cm) between each log of filling. To seal, fold the pasta over the filling to the opposite side and use your index fingers to press down along the sides of the logs of filling, pushing out the air and sealing the pasta. Work your way down the entire length of the sheet, individually sealing each log of filling. Use a spritz of water to help seal it if necessary. Using a fluted pasta wheel, trim the edges, leaving about ¼ inch (6 mm) between the filling and the cut. With the fluted edge facing away from you, place your index fingers on top of the edges and your thumbs behind the filling. Bring the corners close to each other, but not touching. Carefully place the casonsei on the semolina-dusted sheet pans, spaced apart. Bring a large pot of water to a boil. Carefully drop the pasta in the water and cook until al dente, about 2 to 3 minutes.

To serve, divide the pasta between bowls. Garnish with parsley and hazelnuts.

PORK AND PARSNIP TORTELLI WITH APPLES AND WALNUTS

The square tortelli in this recipe are packed with a powerhouse combination of flavors. When choosing a parsnip, be sure to bypass the enormous ones—they make the prep work easier, but they tend to be woody and tough, not tender and sweet, like their smaller counterparts.

SERVES 4–6

FILLING

Olive oil

1 lb (454 g) ground pork

3 garlic cloves, minced

3 parsnips, diced small

Kosher salt

Freshly ground black pepper

1 bunch Italian flat-leaf parsley

½ cup (90 g) grated Pecorino Romano

TORTELLI

Ravioli Dough (page 20)

TO FINISH

½ cup (115 g) unsalted butter

1 tbsp (16 g) whole grain mustard

1 green apple, thinly sliced

½ cup (58 g) walnuts, chopped

To make the filling, in a large sauté pan over high heat, add a drizzle of olive oil, pork, garlic, parsnips, salt and freshly ground black pepper. Cook until the pork is brown and the parsnips are soft, about 6 minutes. Place in a food processor with parsley and Pecorino Romano and pulse until finely ground.

Dust two sheet pans with semolina flour.

To make the pasta, roll out the dough until the sheet is just translucent (see page 17). Cut the rolled-out sheets into 12-inch (30-cm) sections and cover the rest with plastic wrap. Lay the sheets on a dry work surface and, using a straight wheel cutter or a knife, cut the pasta sheets lengthwise into two 3-inch (7.5-cm-) wide strips. Using a piping bag or a spoon, place 1½-inch (3.8-cm) logs of filling down the middle of each sheet in a row, leaving about ½ inch (12 mm) between each log of filling. To seal, fold the pasta over the filling to the opposite side and use your index fingers to press down along the sides of the logs of filling, pushing out the air and sealing the pasta. Work your way down the entire length of the sheet, individually sealing each log of filling. Use a spritz of water to help seal it if necessary. Using a fluted pasta wheel, trim the edges, leaving about ¼ inch (6 mm) between the filling and the cut. Carefully place the tortelli on the semolina-dusted sheet pans, spaced apart.

Bring a large pot of salted water to a boil.

In the meantime, in a large sauté pan, on medium-low heat, add the butter and cook until brown and has a nutty aroma, about 3 to 4 minutes. Remove from the heat, add whole-grain mustard and stir to combine.

Carefully drop the pasta in the water and cook until al dente, about 2 to 3 minutes. Add to the pan with the brown butter and toss to combine.

To finish, divide the pasta between plates. Garnish with thinly sliced green apples and walnuts.

(continued)

Place 1½-inch (3.8-cm) logs of filling down the entire length of dough.

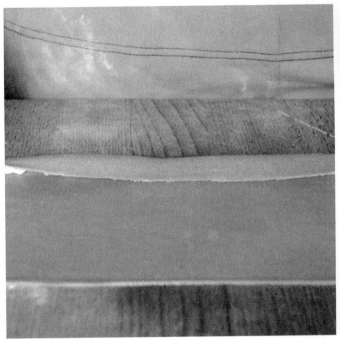

Fold the pasta over the filling and press down to seal.

Using a fluted cutter, trim the edge of the pasta as close to the filling as possible. Then cut between the filling into individual tortelli.

Finished tortelli.

BEET AND ROSE SCARPINOCC WITH POPPY SEEDS

This pasta derived its name from the handmade cloth shoes native to the region of Parre. The soft cheeses in this dish are the ultimate comfort food and balance the tart beets for a satisfying flavor combination.

SERVES 4–6

FILLING
½ cup (115 g) butter

2 lb (907 g) beets

Olive oil

Kosher salt

Freshly ground black pepper

3 tbsp (48 ml) rose water

1½ cups (341 g) mascarpone

1½ cups (341 g) ricotta cheese

SCARPINOCC
Ravioli Dough (page 20)

TO FINISH
½ cup (115 g) unsalted butter

1 tbsp (8 g) poppy seeds

Preheat the oven to 425°F (218°C).

To brown the butter, in a large sauté pan over medium high heat, add butter. Cook until it is brown and has a nutty aroma, about 3 to 4 minutes. Set aside.

To make the filling, toss the beets in olive oil, salt and freshly ground pepper in a large bowl. Put the beets in a baking dish and cover tightly with foil. Roast until tender when pierced with a knife, 45 to 60 minutes depending on their size. Set aside until they are cool enough to peel and chop. Then in a food processor, pulse the beets with rose water and brown butter until combined. Fold in the mascarpone and ricotta in a bowl. Season with salt and freshly ground pepper.

Dust two sheet pans with semolina flour.

To make the pasta, roll out the dough until the sheet is just translucent (see page 17). Cut the rolled-out sheets into 12-inch (30-cm) sections and cover the rest with plastic wrap. Lay the sheets on a dry work surface and, using a straight wheel cutter or a knife, cut the pasta sheets into rectangles 2½ inches (6 cm) long by 2 inches (5 cm) wide. Using a piping bag or a spoon, place 1½-inch (3.8-cm) logs of filling in the middle of the rectangle, leaving about ¼ inch (6 mm) of space on each side. To seal, fold the bottom edge over the filling and carefully roll the pasta away from you to form a tubelike shape. Use a spritz of water to help seal it if necessary. Pinch down the sides, sealing the dough where the filling ends, and use your thumbs to pinch both ends to make a T formation. Gently press into the middle of the filling to create a dimple in the pasta. Carefully place the scarpinocc on the semolina-dusted sheet pans, spaced apart.

Bring a large pot of salted water to a boil. Carefully drop the pasta in the water and cook until al dente, about 2 to 3 minutes. Meanwhile melt butter in a medium sauté pan on medium heat. Add the pasta to the sauté pan and toss to combine.

To serve, divide the pasta between plates. Garnish with poppy seeds.

(continued)

Place the filling down the length of the rectangle close to the edge.

Fold the bottom edge over the filling.

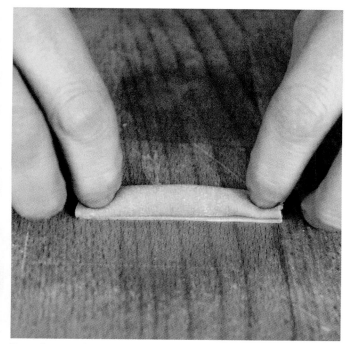

Press down on the opposite ends to seal, using your thumbs to make a T formation. Then gently press into the middle of the filling to create a dimple.

Finished scarpinocc.

CULURGIONES WITH BROWN BUTTER AND ALMONDS

Culurgiones are a traditional ravioli hailing from the island of Sardinia. Their shape, which resembles an ear of wheat, is certainly one of the most difficult to master.

SERVES 4–6

FILLING

1 lb (454 g) Yukon gold potatoes, peeled and quartered

Olive oil

1 egg

1 cup (100 g) grated Pecorino Romano

Kosher salt

Freshly ground black pepper

CULURGIONES

Semolina Dough (page 21)

TO FINISH

½ cup (115 g) butter

¼ cup (43 g) almonds, chopped

Pecorino Romano, for grating

To make the filling, place the potatoes in a large pot. Cover with cold water and season generously with salt. Bring the pot of water to a boil and cook until the potatoes are fork-tender, about 20 to 25 minutes. Drain the potatoes and pass through a food mill or ricer. Once the potatoes are mashed, add the olive oil, egg and Pecorino Romano. Season with salt and freshly ground pepper.

Dust two sheet pans with semolina flour.

To make the pasta, roll out the dough until the sheet is just translucent (see page 17). Cut the rolled-out sheets into 12-inch (30-cm) sections and cover the rest with plastic wrap. Lay the sheets on a dry work surface and, using a round 3-inch (7.5-cm) cutter, cut circles into the sheet. Using a piping bag or a spoon, place about 1 tablespoon (15 g) of filling in the middle of the pasta circle, leaving about 1-inch (2.5-cm) around the sides. To shape, holding the filled pasta round in your hand like a taco, begin pinching the dough together at the bottom, pushing upward as you pinch the next section, working your way to the other end. Carefully transfer the culurgiones to the semolina-dusted sheet pans, spaced apart.

Bring a large pot of salted water to a boil. Carefully drop the pasta in the water and cook until al dente, about 2 to 3 minutes.

To brown the butter, in a large sauté pan over medium-high heat, add butter. Cook until it is brown and has a nutty aroma, about 3 to 4 minutes. Toss the pasta in the brown butter.

To serve, divide the pasta between bowls. Garnish with almonds and grated Pecorino Romano.

CHAPTER FIVE

CUT PASTA

Harness your flour power in this chapter—pretty much all you need is a steady hand and a sharp knife. The recipes that follow in this chapter are me once again riffing on the common theme of the doughs we mastered in the first chapter. Here, the pasta is shaped with the use of a knife, versus by hand, as in previous chapters. The benefit to cutting the pasta in this way is a precision in proportions and measurement of each noodle that finish in more ribbon-like, more consistent pasta dishes. Some of the more delicate and labor-intensive recipes can be found in this chapter, and I guarantee that the precision and exactitude of the pasta will be well balanced in the variety and interpretation of the sauces and pasta pairings throughout the chapter.

ROASTED GARLIC FETTUCCINE WITH RAZOR CLAMS AND BACCALA

This recipe is a great way to serve up freshly dug (or bought) clams. Baccala, or salted cod, is traditionally served on Christmas Eve tables across Italy as part of the Feast of the Seven Fishes.

SERVES 4–6

PARMIGIANO-REGGIANO BROTH

1 lb (454 g) Parmigiano-Reggiano rinds

1 tbsp black peppercorns

2 qt (1.9 L) water

ROASTED GARLIC FETTUCCINE

1 bulb garlic

Olive oil

Egg Dough (page 19)

RAZOR CLAMS

Olive oil

1 bulb fennel, sliced

1 onion, diced small

2 garlic cloves, minced

4 lb (1.8 kg) razor clams

4 oz (113 g) baccala

1 cup (237 ml) white wine

1 bunch dill, chopped

Kosher salt

Freshly ground black pepper

TO FINISH

Italian bread

Extra-virgin olive oil

To make the broth, add the Parmigiano-Reggiano rinds and peppercorns to water in a large saucepot on medium-high heat. Bring to a boil. Reduce the heat and simmer, stirring occasionally to prevent the cheese from sticking to the bottom of pot. Cook until the broth is flavorful and reduced by half, about 2 hours.

Preheat the oven to 400°F (204°C). Cut the top off of the entire bulb of garlic. Place on a piece of aluminum foil and drizzle with olive oil. Roast for about 45 minutes. Allow to cool and then squeeze the cloves into a bowl and mash. Dust two sheet pans with semolina flour.

To make the roasted garlic dough, follow the instructions for Egg Dough, incorporating the mashed roasted garlic with the wet ingredients. To make the pasta, roll out the dough until the sheet is about 1⁄16-inch (1.6-mm) thick (see page 17). Cut the rolled-out sheets into 12-inch (30-cm) sections and, working in batches, stack about 4 sheets on top of one another, generously dusting semolina between the layers. Fold the dough over to the middle and then again to the other end, like a letter, to form 3 layers. Using a knife, cut the folded dough into 1⁄4-inch (6-mm) strips. With your hands, shake off the semolina and form the pasta into small nests. Place the fettuccine on the semolina-dusted sheet pans.

Bring a large pot of water to a boil.

To cook the seafood, in a large sauté pan on medium-high heat, drizzle the olive oil. Add the fennel, onion and garlic and cook until tender, about 5 to 8 minutes. Add the razor clams, baccala and white wine. Cook for about 5 to 8 minutes, until the wine is reduced and the alcohol is cooked out. Add the dill and season with salt and freshly ground black pepper.

Carefully drop the pasta in the water and cook until al dente, about 2 to 3 minutes. Then add the cooked pasta to the seafood and toss to combine.

To serve, divide the pasta between bowls. Ladle the broth on the pasta. Garnish with a piece of crusty Italian bread and a drizzle of extra-virgin olive oil.

(continued)

Generously dust the dough sheet with semolina.

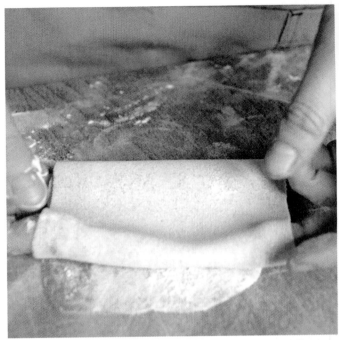

Fold the dough over to the middle and then again to the end, like a letter.

Using a sharp knife, cut the dough into ¼-inch (6-mm) strips.

Finished fettuccine.

FARFALLE WITH ROASTED TOMATOES AND CHILE

Often known as bowtie pasta, *farfalle* is literally translated to "butterflies," which I think is much nicer. Keep in mind, you have a lot of room for trial and error with the twists; the more creative the shapes, the more visually exciting the dish.

SERVES 4–6

FARFALLE

Egg Dough (page 19)

ROASTED TOMATOES AND CHILE

Olive oil

1 garlic clove, thinly sliced

1 lb (454 g) Roma tomatoes, halved lengthwise

1 Calabrian chile, thinly sliced

Kosher salt

Freshly ground black pepper

TO FINISH

Extra-virgin olive oil

Pecorino Romano, for grating

Basil, torn

Dust two sheet pans with semolina flour.

To make the pasta, roll out the dough until the sheet is about 1/16-inch (1.6-mm) thick (see page 17). Cut the rolled-out sheets into 12-inch (30-cm) sections and cover the rest with plastic wrap. Using a straight wheel cutter, cut the sheets lengthwise into 1½-inch (4-cm-) wide strips. Then cut across the strips every 2 inches (5 cm), creating rectangles. With the rectangle flat on the table, place your index finger down in the middle and your thumb and middle finger on opposite sides on the dough. Then bring your thumb and middle finger together to your index finger, gently pinching the bunched up dough to form the bowtie shape. Carefully place the farfalle on the semolina-dusted sheet pans, spaced apart.

Bring a large pot of salted water to a boil.

In a large sauté pan, over high heat, add a drizzle of olive oil, garlic, tomatoes and chile. Season with salt and freshly ground black pepper. Reduce the heat to low and keep warm while you cook the pasta. Carefully drop the pasta into the boiling water and cook until al dente, about 2 to 3 minutes. Add the pasta to the pan with the tomatoes and toss to combine.

To serve, divide the pasta between bowls. Garnish with a drizzle of extra-virgin olive oil, grated Pecorino Romano and some torn basil.

(continued)

Cut the pasta sheet lengthwise into 1½-inch (4-cm) wide strips.

Then cut across the strips every 2 inches (5 cm) creating rectangles.

Place your index finder in the middle of the rectangle, and your thumb and middle finger on opposite sides. Bring your thumb and middle finger together pinching the dough to seal it.

Finished farfalle.

TAGLIATELLE PRIMAVERA

This is one of the more New York–inspired dishes in the book, after Sirio Maccioni of Le Cirque fame. It is both simple and elegant, and the most "Tuscan" part of the dish is the use of fresh, seasonal ingredients—feel free to improvise with whatever looks good at the farmers market today.

SERVES 4–6

TAGLIATELLE
Egg Dough (page 19)

PRIMAVERA
Olive oil

2 garlic cloves, thinly sliced

1 red onion, thinly sliced

1 green zucchini, diced small

1 summer squash, diced small

1 red pepper, diced small

8 oz (227 g) cherry tomatoes, halved

1 bunch asparagus, sliced on the bias into 1-inch (2.5-cm) pieces

1 lb (454 g) spinach

Kosher salt

Freshly ground black pepper

TO FINISH
Extra-virgin olive oil

1 lemon, zested

Parmigiano-Reggiano, for grating

Dust two sheet pans with semolina flour.

To make the pasta, roll out the dough until the sheet is about 1⁄16-inch (1.6-mm) thick (see page 17). Cut the rolled-out sheets into 12-inch (30-cm) sections and, working in batches, stack about 4 sheets on top of one another, generously dusting semolina between the layers. Fold the dough over to the middle and then again to the other end, like a letter, to form 3 layers. Using a knife, cut the folded dough into 1⁄4-inch (6-mm) wide strips. With your hands, shake off the semolina and form the pasta into small nests. Place the tagliatelle on the semolina-dusted sheet pans.

Bring a large pot of salted water to a boil.

In a large sauté pan, add a drizzle of olive oil, garlic, red onion, zucchini, summer squash, pepper, tomatoes and asparagus. Cook until tender, about 5 minutes, and then add the spinach. Season with salt and freshly ground black pepper. Carefully drop the pasta into the boiling water and cook until al dente, about 2 to 3 minutes. Add the pasta to the pan with all of the vegetables and toss to combine.

To serve, divide the pasta between bowls. Garnish with some extra-virgin olive oil, lemon zest and grated Parmigiano-Reggiano.

INK SPAGHETTI ALLA CHITARRA WITH CURED YOLK AND POACHED EGG

This spaghetti dish is an instant crowd-pleaser, with the color contrast between the egg and the dark pasta. The rough and porous texture of the spaghetti combined with the hearty poached egg makes for a satisfying year-round pasta dish. The cured yolk is a weeklong process that is well worth the wait.

SERVES 4–6

CURED YOLK

3½ cups (868 g) kosher salt

3 tbsp ground black pepper

2 sprigs thyme

1 sprig rosemary

3 egg yolks

INK SPAGHETTI

Egg Dough (page 19)

3 tbsp (48 ml) squid ink

POACHED EGG

1 tbsp (16 ml) vinegar

4–6 eggs

TO FINISH

Extra-virgin olive oil

Crushed red pepper, to taste

Kosher salt

Freshly ground black pepper

To make the cured yolks, mix together the salt, pepper, thyme and rosemary in a mixing bowl. Then in a container with a flat bottom, add about three quarters of the salt mixture. With your hands, make individual wells for the yolks. Carefully place the yolks in the salt and cover with the remaining salt mixture. Cover the container and put in the refrigerator for 3 days. After 3 days, the yolk should be somewhat firm to the touch. Carefully remove them from the salt and brush off the excess. Place the yolks individually in a piece of cheesecloth or on a rack to dry out for another 3 days in the refrigerator.

To make the squid ink spaghetti, follow the instructions for Egg Dough, incorporating the squid ink with the wet ingredients. To make the pasta, roll out the dough until the sheet is about ⅟₁₆-inch (1.6-mm) thick (see page 17).

Dust two sheet pans with semolina flour.

If you are cutting the dough with a chitarra, cut the rolled-out sections into the same length as your chitarra. Generously dust both sides of the dough and the top of the strings with semolina. Using a rolling pin, lightly press the dough to set it in place so it won't slide off. Then, press down with more force to cut the dough through the strings into spaghetti. Shake off the excess semolina and form into small nests. Place the spaghetti on the semolina-dusted sheet pans.

If you are cutting the spaghetti by hand, cut the rolled-out sheets into 12-inch (30-cm) sections and, working in batches, stack about 4 sheets on top of one another, generously dusting semolina between the layers. Fold the dough over to the middle and then again to the other end, like a letter, to form 3 layers. Using a knife, cut the folded dough into ⅟₁₆-inch (1.6-mm) thick strips (about the same size as the dough's thickness). With your hands, shake off the semolina and form into small nests. Place the spaghetti on the semolina-dusted sheet pan.

(continued)

INK SPAGHETTI ALLA CHITARRA WITH CURED YOLK AND POACHED EGG (CONT.)

Bring a large pot of salted water to a boil. In the meantime, begin poaching the eggs. In a medium saucepan, bring water to a boil with the vinegar. Reduce to a low simmer and slowly swirl the water to create a whirlpool. Working in batches, crack the egg into the water and allow to cook for about 3 minutes or until the white is somewhat firm. Carefully remove with a slotted spoon and drain on a paper towel. Once all of the eggs are cooked, drop the pasta in the boiling water.

In a large sauté pan, add the olive oil and crushed red pepper. Add the cooked pasta to the pan and toss to combine. Season with salt and freshly ground black pepper.

To serve, divide between bowls. Carefully place the poached egg on top of the pasta. Garnish with extra-virgin olive oil and grated cured egg yolk.

PAPPARDELLE WITH WILD MUSHROOM BOLOGNESE

The name *pappardelle* is derived from the Italian *pappare*, "to gobble up." And gobble you shall. This Tuscan dish is a vegetarian gem and a fall favorite.

SERVES 4–6

WILD MUSHROOM BOLOGNESE

Olive oil

3 garlic cloves, thinly sliced

2 carrots, diced small

2 stalks celery, diced small

1 onion, diced small

3 lb (1.4 kg) wild mushrooms, diced small

Kosher salt

Freshly ground black pepper

3 tbsp (48 g) tomato paste

1 cup (237 ml) red wine

1 (28-oz [794-g]) can crushed tomatoes

1 bunch thyme

1 bunch Italian flat-leaf parsley, chopped

PAPPARDELLE

Egg Dough (page 19)

TO FINISH

Parmigiano-Reggiano, for grating

Basil, thinly sliced

To make the mushroom Bolognese, in a large pot over medium heat, add a drizzle of olive oil. Then add the garlic, carrots, celery, onion and mushrooms. Season with salt and freshly ground black pepper and cook until soft, about 4 minutes. Add the tomato paste and cook for about a minute, stirring frequently. Add the red wine and let it reduce by half, about 2 minutes. Then add the crushed tomatoes, thyme and chopped parsley. Reduce the heat to low and allow to cook for about 45 minutes.

Dust two sheet pans with semolina flour.

To make the pasta, roll out the dough until the sheet is about 1/16-inch (1.6-mm) thick (see page 17). Cut the rolled-out sheets into 12-inch (30-cm) sections and, working in batches, stack about 4 sheets on top of one another, generously dusting semolina between the layers. Fold the dough over to the middle and then again to the other end, like a letter, to form 3 layers. Using a knife, cut the folded dough into 1-inch (2.5-cm) strips. With your hands, shake off the semolina and form the pasta into small nests. Place the pappardelle on the semolina-dusted sheet pans.

Bring a large pot of salted water to a boil.

In a large sauté pan, over medium heat, add a drizzle of olive oil and some mushroom Bolognese. Carefully drop the pasta into the boiling water and cook until al dente, about 2 to 3 minutes. Add the pasta to the pan with the sauce and toss to combine.

To serve, divide the pasta between bowls. Garnish with grated Parmigiano-Reggiano and basil.

(continued)

Using a sharp knife, cut the folded dough into 1-inch (2.5-cm) strips.

Cut pappardelle pasta.

Carefully separate the pasta and generously dust with semonlina to prevent from sticking together.

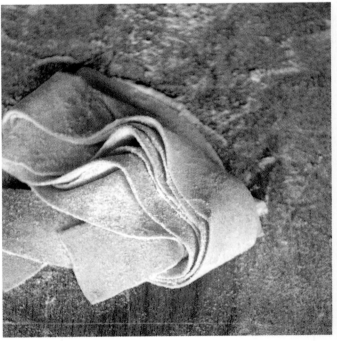

Finished pappardelle.

COCOA MAFALDINE WITH QUAIL AND WALNUTS

Translated to "little queens" pasta, this fancy, scalloped-edged recipe pairs the delicate nature of the ruffled pasta with a light ragu sauce for a sophisticated and elegant dinner.

SERVES 4–6

QUAIL RAGU

4 quail, deboned

Kosher salt

Freshly ground black pepper

Olive oil

1 carrot, diced small

2 celery stalks, diced small

1 onion, diced small

3 garlic cloves, minced

8 oz (227 g) cherry tomatoes

2 tbsp (32 g) tomato paste

1 cup (237 ml) red wine

2 cups (472 ml) chicken stock

1 bay leaf

1 bunch thyme

MAFALDINE

Egg dough (page 19)

3 tbsp (21 g) cocoa powder

TO FINISH

1 bunch chives, thinly sliced

½ cup (58 g) walnuts, roughly chopped

Preheat the oven to 350°F (177°C).

To make the quail ragu, generously season the quail with salt and freshly ground black pepper. In a large Dutch oven, over high heat, add a drizzle of olive oil and the quail. Brown on all sides, about 2 minutes per side. Set aside. In the same pot, add a drizzle of olive oil, carrot, celery, onion, garlic and tomatoes. Cook until soft, about 2 minutes. Then add the tomato paste and cook for about 1 minute, stirring frequently. Add the red wine and let it reduce by half, about 2 minutes. Add the chicken stock, bay leaf and thyme and season with salt and freshly ground black pepper. Return the quail to the Dutch oven and bring up to a boil. Cover and place in the oven. Cook for about 2 hours or until the meat is fork-tender. Remove the bay leaf before serving.

Dust two sheet pans with semolina flour.

To make the cocoa dough, follow the instructions for Egg Dough, incorporating the cocoa powder with the dry ingredients.

To make the pasta, roll out the dough until the sheet is just translucent (see page 17). Cut the rolled-out sheets into 12-inch (30-cm) sections and cover the rest with plastic wrap. Lay the sheets on a dry work surface and using a fluted cutter, cut the pasta sheets lengthwise into ¼-inch (6-mm) strips. With your hands, shake off the semolina and place the mafaldine on the semolina-dusted sheet pans.

Bring a large pot of salted water to a boil.

In a large sauté pan, over medium heat, add some of the quail ragu. Carefully drop the pasta in the boiling water and cook until al dente, about 2 to 3 minutes. Add the cooked pasta to the ragu and toss to combine.

To serve, divide the pasta between bowls. Garnish with chives and chopped walnuts.

HERB FETTUCCINE WITH MUSSELS AND SPECK

One of the easier pasta dishes in this chapter, the smokiness of the speck, from the Tyrol region, dominates the full-bodied flavor in this recipe. Espelette peppers can be purchased as festoons of dry or fresh peppers, pickled in jars, pureed or as ground pepper.

SERVES 4–6

HERB FETTUCCINE

½ cup (118 ml) olive oil

1 bunch Italian flat-leaf parsley

1 bunch dill

1 bunch tarragon

Egg Dough (page 19)

STEAMED MUSSELS

Olive oil

3 garlic cloves, thinly sliced

3 lb (1.4 kg) mussels

2 cups (472 ml) white wine

TO FINISH

Olive oil

4 oz (113 g) speck, cut into ½-inch (12-mm) pieces

Kosher salt

Freshly ground black pepper

Espelette pepper, to taste

Italian flat-leaf parsley, picked

In a food processor, add the olive oil, parsley, dill and tarragon. Process until completely smooth.

To make the herb dough, follow the instructions for Egg Dough (page 19), incorporating the pureed herbs with the wet ingredients.

Dust two sheet pans with semolina flour.

To make the pasta, roll out the dough until the sheet is about ¹⁄₁₆-inch (1.6-mm) thick (see page 17). Cut the rolled-out sheets into 12-inch (30-cm) sections and, working in batches, stack about 4 sheets on top of one another, generously dusting semolina between the layers. Fold the dough over to the middle and then again to the other end, like a letter, to form 3 layers. Using a knife, cut the folded dough into ¼-inch (6-mm) strips. With your hands, shake off the semolina and form the pasta into small nests. Place the fettuccine on the semolina-dusted sheet pans.

In a large pot, over high heat, add a drizzle of olive oil and the garlic. Then add the mussels and white wine. Cover and allow the mussels to steam, about 5 to 6 minutes. Once all of the shells open, remove from the heat and allow to cool. Remove the meat from the shells and reserve.

Bring a large pot of salted water to a boil.

In a large sauté pan, over medium-high heat, add a drizzle of olive oil and the speck. Cook for about 3 minutes and then drop the pasta in the boiling water. Cook until al dente, about 2 to 3 minutes. Add the pasta to the sauté pan with the mussels and toss to combine. Season with salt and freshly ground black pepper.

To serve, divide the pasta between bowls. Garnish with Espelette pepper and parsley.

PIZZOCCHERI WITH SWISS CHARD, FINGERLINGS AND GRANA PADANA

Guaranteed to impress even the most discerning Italophiles (or Italian grandmothers), this dish from the Lombardy region is a rare find on a menu in North America. Aside from just making you feel fancy, the unique bite of the pasta is a nice foray into the culinary unknown for many non-Italian chefs.

SERVES 4–6

PIZZOCCHERI

1 cup (120 g) buckwheat flour

2¼ cups (286 g) 00 flour

1 tbsp (16 g) kosher salt

14 egg yolks

2 tsp extra-virgin olive oil

TO FINISH

1 lb (454 g) fingerling potatoes

2 sprigs rosemary

Olive oil

1 bunch Swiss chard, ribs removed, cut into pieces

1 garlic clove, minced

Kosher salt

Freshly ground black pepper

¼ cup (58 g) unsalted butter

Grana Padano, for grating

To make the pizzoccheri dough, mix the buckwheat flour, 00 flour and salt on a dry work surface. Form a mound about 10 inches (25 cm) in diameter. Using your hands, create a well in the middle of the flour-and-salt mixture. Slowly pour the egg yolks and oil into the middle and gently beat. Gradually work the flour in using your fingers or a fork. Combine the flour, egg yolks and oil until fully incorporated. If the dough is sticking to your work surface, add a little bit of flour. If the dough feels dry, spray a little bit of water to bind it together. Once the dough is formed into a ball, begin to knead it by pushing down with the heel of your hand and rotating it. Knead the dough for about 10 to 15 minutes. The dough has had sufficient kneading when it has a smooth appearance and springs back when you press it. Wrap the dough tightly with plastic wrap and let it rest for at least 30 minutes at room temperature before using.

In a medium saucepan, over high heat, add the fingerlings and rosemary with enough water to cover them. Bring to a boil. Cook until the potatoes are partially cooked, about 8 to 10 minutes. Allow them to cool and then slice in half lengthwise.

Dust two sheet pans with semolina flour. To make the pasta, roll out the dough until the sheet is about ¹⁄₁₆ inch (1.6-mm) thick (see page 17). Cut the rolled-out sheets into 12-inch (30-cm) sections and working in batches stack about 4 sheets on top of one another, generously dusting semolina between the layers. Using a straight wheel cutter, cut the stacked dough into ½-inch (12-mm) by 3-inch (7.5-cm) strips. Place the pizzoccheri on the semolina-dusted sheet pans.

Bring a large pot of salted water to a boil. In the meantime, in a large sauté pan, over medium-high heat, add a drizzle of olive oil and the sliced fingerlings (cut side down). Allow the potatoes to brown, about 2 minutes, then add the Swiss chard and garlic. Season with salt and freshly ground black pepper. Reduce the heat to low and drop the pasta into the boiling water. Cook until al dente, about 1 to 2 minutes. Add the pasta to the pan with the Swiss chard and toss to combine. Add the butter and grate in some Grana Padano. To serve, divide between bowls. Garnish with more grated Grana Padano.

TAGLIARINI WITH CERIGNOLA OLIVES AND LEMON

Tagliarini is often associated in certain parts of Italy with Carnivale and the start of Lent. Cerignola olives, among the biggest and most attractive Italian olives, balance nicely with the delicate ribbon of the pasta.

SERVES 4–6

TAGLIARINI
Egg Dough (page 19)

OLIVE TAPENADE
Olive oil

1 garlic clove, minced

1 cup (180 g) Cerignola olives, pitted, chopped

4 anchovy fillets, minced

¼ cup (60 g) capers, chopped

1 bunch parsley, chopped

Kosher salt

Freshly ground black pepper

TO FINISH
¼ cup (45 g) grated Parmigiano-Reggiano

Extra-virgin olive oil

1 lemon, zested

Dust two sheet pans with semolina flour.

To make the pasta, roll out the dough until the sheet is about ⅟₁₆-inch (1.6-mm) thick (see page 17). Cut the rolled-out sheets into 12-inch (30-cm) sections and, working in batches, stack about 4 sheets on top of one another, generously dusting semolina between the layers. Fold the dough over to the middle and then again to the other end, like a letter, to form 3 layers. Using a knife, cut the folded dough into ⅛-inch (3-mm) strips. With your hands, shake off the semolina and form the pasta into small nests. Place the tagliarini on the semolina-dusted sheet pans.

Bring a large pot of salted water to a boil.

In a large sauté pan, over medium heat, add a drizzle of olive oil, garlic, olives, anchovies, capers, parsley, salt and pepper and stir to combine. Carefully drop the pasta in the boiling water and cook until al dente, about 2 to 3 minutes. Add the pasta to the sauté pan with grated Parmigiano-Reggiano and toss to combine.

To serve, divide between bowls. Garnish with extra-virgin olive oil and lemon zest.

SPAGHETTI CACIO E PEPE

One of the more traditional Roman recipes, this spaghetti dish of literally "cheese and pepper" keeps it relatively simple, focusing all the flavor on the salty Pecorino Romano cheese and the cracked black pepper finish.

SERVES 4–6

SPAGHETTI
Egg Dough (page 19)

TO FINISH
½ cup (115 g) unsalted butter

Freshly ground black pepper

¾ cup (75 g) grated Pecorino Romano, plus more for garnish

Extra-virgin olive oil

Dust two sheet pans with semolina flour.

To make the pasta, roll out the dough until the sheet is about ¹⁄₁₆-inch (1.6-mm) thick (see page 17). Cut the rolled-out sheets into 12-inch (30-cm) sections and, working in batches, stack about 4 sheets on top of one another, generously dusting semolina between the layers. Fold the dough over to the middle and then again to the other end, like a letter, to form 3 layers. Using a knife, cut the folded dough into ¹⁄₁₆-inch (1.6-mm) thick strips (about the same size as the dough's thickness). With your hands, shake off the semolina and form the pasta into small nests. Place the spaghetti on the semolina-dusted sheet pans.

Bring a large pot of salted water to a boil.

In a large sauté pan, over medium-high heat, add the butter and melt. In the meantime, carefully drop the pasta into the boiling water and cook until al dente, about 2 to 3 minutes. Add the pasta to the pan with the butter and toss to combine. Season generously with freshly ground black pepper and grated Pecorino Romano.

To serve, divide the pasta between bowls. Garnish with olive oil and more grated Pecorino Romano.

CHESTNUT STRACCI WITH BRAISED PORK RIBS AND PEARS

This "rag" pasta is one of the most fun to make because the loosely cut or torn pasta pieces can be imperfect. The braised ribs in this dish create a juicy, succulent pairing.

SERVES 4–6

BRAISED PORK RIBS

4 lb (1.8 kg) pork ribs

Kosher salt

Freshly ground black pepper

Olive oil

2 pears, diced small

3 garlic cloves, chopped

1 onion, diced small

2 carrots, diced small

2 celery stalks, diced small

1 cup (237 ml) chicken stock

1 (28-oz [794-g]) can crushed tomatoes

1 bunch Italian flat-leaf parsley, chopped

STRACCI

Egg Dough (page 19)

3 tbsp (17 g) chestnut flour

TO FINISH

Olive oil

Italian flat-leaf parsley, chopped

Parmigiano-Reggiano, for grating

Preheat the oven to 375°F (190°C).

To make the braised pork ribs, generously season the ribs with salt and freshly ground black pepper. In a large Dutch oven, over high heat, add a drizzle of olive oil. Working in batches, brown the ribs, about 2 minutes on each side, and set aside. Add another drizzle of olive oil, the pears, garlic, onion, carrots and celery and cook until soft, about 3 to 4 minutes. Then add the chicken stock, tomatoes and parsley. Season with salt and freshly ground black pepper. Cover and place in the oven. Cook for about 2 hours or until the meat is falling off the bone. Allow to cool, and discard the ribs. Keep warm.

Dust two sheet pans with semolina flour.

To make the chestnut dough, follow the instructions for Egg Dough, incorporating the chestnut flour with the dry ingredients.

To make the pasta, roll out the dough until the the sheet is about 1/16-inch (1.6-mm) thick (see page 17). Cut the rolled out sheets into 12-inch (30-cm) sections and cover the rest with plastic wrap. Lay the sheets on a dry work surface and using a straight wheel cutter or a knife, cut the pasta sheets into 2-inch (5-cm) squares. Carefully place the Stracci on the semolina-dusted sheet pans, spaced apart.

Bring a large pot of salted water to a boil.

In a large sauté pan, over medium-high heat, add a drizzle of olive oil and some of the braised pork rib ragu. Carefully drop the pasta into the boiling water and cook until al dente, about 2 to 3 minutes. Add the pasta to the pan with the pork and toss to combine.

To serve, divide the pasta between bowls. Garnish with parsley and grated Parmigiano-Reggiano.

HERB GARGANELLI WITH ARTICHOKES AND MEYER LEMON

This penne-with-a-flap pasta is another solid vegetarian pasta dish. When selecting the artichokes for this recipe (and anytime you select an artichoke), look for tightly packed leaves; splayed leaves are a sign the artichoke is not the freshest.

SERVES 4–6

HERB GARGANELLI

½ cup (118 ml) olive oil

1 bunch Italian flat-leaf parsley

1 bunch dill

1 bunch tarragon

Egg Dough (page 19)

BRAISED ARTICHOKES

2 lemons, 1 juiced, 1 zested

4 medium artichokes

¼ cup (59 ml) olive oil

1 onion, diced

2 garlic cloves, smashed

1 bunch parsley

1 cup (237 ml) white wine

1 cup (237 ml) chicken stock

½ cup (115 g) unsalted butter

TO FINISH

Olive oil

1 garlic clove, thinly sliced

1 Meyer lemon, juice and zest

Kosher salt

Freshly ground black pepper

Pecorino Romano, for grating

In a food processor, add the olive oil, parsley, dill and tarragon. Process until completely smooth. To make the herb garganelli, follow the instructions for Egg Dough, incorporating the pureed greens with the wet ingredients.

Dust two sheet pans with semolina flour. To make the pasta, roll out the dough until the sheet is about 1⁄16-inch (1.6-mm) thick (see page 17). Cut the rolled-out sheets into 12-inch (30-cm) sections and cover the rest with plastic wrap. Lay the sheets on a dry work surface and, using a straight wheel cutter or a knife, cut the pasta sheets into 2-inch (5-cm) squares. Place the cut square on your garganelli board diagonally so that it resembles a diamond. Place the wooden dowel at the bottom of the diamond and curl it over the top. Using gentle pressure, roll the dowel away from you to form the tube-like garganelli shape. Place the pasta on the semolina-dusted sheet pans, spaced apart.

To braise the artichokes, fill a large bowl with water and the juice of 1 lemon, tossing in the lemon halves as well. Rinse each artichoke and trim ½ inch (12 mm) off the stalk. Trim 1 inch (2.5 cm) off the top of each artichoke. Then cut each artichoke in half, from stalk to tip, and remove the choke with a spoon. Remove the tough outer leaves and trim the outside of the stalk with a paring knife. Add the prepared artichokes to the bowl of lemon water to keep it from browning. In a large saucepan over medium heat, add the olive oil, onion, garlic and parsley and cook for about 3 minutes or until translucent. Add the cleaned artichokes and white wine. Allow the white wine to reduce by half, about 2 minutes. Add the chicken stock, zest of 1 lemon and butter; cover and cook for about 20 minutes on low heat, until tender.

Bring a large pot of salted water to a boil. In a large sauté pan, over medium-high heat, add a drizzle of olive oil, garlic and braised artichokes. Carefully drop the pasta into the boiling water and cook until al dente, about 2 to 3 minutes. Add the cooked pasta to the pan with lemon juice and toss to combine. Season with salt and freshly ground black pepper.

To serve, divide the pasta between plates. Garnish with lemon zest and grated Pecorino Romano.

CAPPELLACCI DEI BRIGANTI WITH EGGPLANT CAPONATA

The shape of this pasta was modeled after the types of hats that outlaws and other nefarious characters wear. Also referred to as "Badass Pasta" (by me), this foray into culinary haberdashery is one of the harder cut pastas, and one of the most unique.

SERVES 4–6

BRIGANTI
Egg Dough (page 19)

EGGPLANT CAPONATA
Olive oil

1 onion, diced small

1 garlic clove, minced

1 large eggplant, peeled and diced

3 tbsp (48 g) tomato paste

3 tbsp (45 g) capers, chopped

1 bunch Italian flat-leaf parsley

Kosher salt

Freshly ground black pepper

TO FINISH
¼ cup (32 g) pignoli nuts, toasted

Basil, torn

Parmigiano-Reggiano, for grating

Dust two sheet pans with semolina flour.

To make the pasta, roll out the dough until the sheet is about ⅟₁₆-inch (1.6-mm) thick (see page 17). Cut the rolled-out sheets into 12-inch (30-cm) sections and cover the rest with plastic wrap. Lay the sheets on a dry work surface and, using a round 2-inch (5-cm) cutter, cut circles into the sheet. To form the pasta, wrap each round of pasta dough around your index finger to form an open-tipped cone. Seal the pasta on the edges and gently curl up the bottom of the pasta. Carefully transfer the cappellacci dei briganti to the semolina-dusted sheet pans, standing upright and spaced apart.

To make the eggplant caponata, in a large sauté pan, over medium-low heat, add a drizzle of olive oil, onion, garlic and eggplant. Cook until the eggplant is very soft and breaking apart, about 6 to 8 minutes. Then add the tomato paste, capers and parsley and season with salt and freshly ground black pepper. Keep warm.

Bring a large pot of salted water to a boil. Carefully drop the pasta into the boiling water and cook until al dente, about 2 to 3 minutes. Add the pasta to the pan with the caponata and some of the pasta water. Stir to combine.

To serve, divide the pasta between bowls. Garnish with pignoli nuts, basil and grated Parmigiano-Reggiano.

INK FARFALLE WITH OCTOPUS, CALABRIAN CHILES AND CHICKPEAS

This recipe breaks down some of the more traditional flavors we usually associate with these ingredients and throws them back together in an exciting new way.

SERVES 4–6

FARFALLE

Egg Dough (page 19)

3 tbsp (48 ml) squid ink

BRAISED OCTOPUS

1 (3-lb [1.4-kg]) octopus

¼ cup (59 ml) olive oil

1 onion, quartered

1 garlic clove

1 bunch parsley

1 cup (237 ml) white wine

2 bay leaves

3 tomatoes, chopped

TO FINISH

Olive oil

1 bulb fennel, thinly sliced, fronds reserved

1 Calabrian chile, thinly sliced

1 (15.5-oz [440-g]) can chickpeas

Kosher salt

Freshly ground black pepper

1 lemon, juice and zest

To make the squid ink dough, follow the instructions for Egg Dough, incorporating the squid ink with the wet ingredients. To make the pasta, roll out the dough until the sheet is about ¹⁄₁₆-inch (1.6-mm) thick (see page 17).

Dust two sheet pans with semolina flour.

To make the pasta, cut the rolled-out sheets into 12-inch (30-cm) sections and cover the rest with plastic wrap. Using a straight wheel cutter, cut the sheets lengthwise into 1½-inch (3.8-cm-) wide strips. Then cut across the strips every 2 inches (5 cm), creating rectangles. With the rectangle flat on the table, place your index finger down in the middle and your thumb and middle finger on opposite sides on the dough. Then bring your thumb and middle finger together to your index finger, gently pinching the bunched-up dough to form the bowtie shape. Carefully place them on the semolina-dusted sheet pans, spaced apart.

To braise the octopus, in a large pot, over high heat, add the octopus, olive oil, onion, garlic, parsley, white wine, bay leaves and tomatoes. Lower the heat, cover and allow it to cook until tender, about 1½ to 2 hours. Cut the cooled octopus into pieces. Remove the bay leaf before serving.

Bring a large pot of salted water to a boil.

In a large cast-iron pan, over high heat, add a drizzle of olive oil and the cut octopus. Char the octopus, cooking for about 1 minute on each side. Set aside. In the same pan, over medium heat, add a drizzle of olive oil, fennel, chile and chickpeas. Season with salt and freshly ground black pepper.

Carefully add the pasta to the boiling water and cook until al dente, about 2 to 3 minutes. Add the cooked pasta to the pan with the chickpeas and toss to combine. Place the charred octopus back in the pan and toss.

To serve, divide the pasta between plates. Garnish with lemon juice and lemon zest.

MINT CORZETTI WITH LAMB SAUSAGE AND BROCCOLI RABE

This Ligurian pasta dish is a great formal dinner recipe; originally embossed with a wooden hand tool, corzetti was "pressed" as a way for the pasta to better hold its sauce. In this recipe, the light sauce adheres well to the thin rounds of pasta, and the mint adds a delicate finish.

SERVES 4-6

MINT CORZETTI

1 bunch mint

1 cup (237 ml) white wine

3 cups (381 g) 00 flour

2 eggs

TO FINISH

Olive oil

1 lb (454 g) lamb sausage, removed from casing

3 garlic cloves, minced

1 lb (454 g) broccoli rabe, chopped

Lemon, juice and zest

Crushed red pepper, to taste

Kosher salt

Freshly ground black pepper

To make the mint corzetti dough, combine the mint and white wine in a food processor and pulse until smooth. Place the 00 flour on a dry work surface. Form a mound about 10 inches (25 cm) in diameter. Using your hands, create a well in the middle of the flour. Slowly pour the eggs and mint/wine emulsion into the middle and gently beat. Gradually work the flour in, using your fingers or a fork. Combine the flour and egg mixture until it is fully incorporated. If the dough is sticking to your work surface, add a little bit of flour. If the dough feels dry, spray a little bit of water to bind it together.

Once the dough is formed into a ball, begin to knead it by pushing down with the heel of your hand and rotating it. Knead the dough for about 10 to 15 minutes. The dough has had sufficient kneading when it has a smooth appearance and springs back when you press it. Wrap the dough tightly with plastic wrap and let it rest for at least 30 minutes at room temperature before using.

Dust two sheet pans with semolina flour. To make the corzetti, roll out the dough until the sheet is about 1/16-inch (1.6-mm) thick (see page 17). Cut the rolled-out sheets into 12-inch (30-cm) sections and cover the rest with plastic wrap. Lay the sheets on a dry work surface and, using a corzetti stamp, cut out the dough into rounds using the bottom part of the stamp. Place the cut round between the two parts of the stamp and apply light pressure. If you don't have a corzetti stamp, you can just use a 2-inch (5-cm) round cutter to cut circles. Carefully place the corzetti on the semolina-dusted sheet pans and leave it uncovered until ready to cook.

Bring a large pot of salted water to a boil. In a large sauté pan, over medium-high heat, add a drizzle of olive oil, lamb sausage and garlic. Cook until brown, about 5 to 6 minutes. Add the broccoli rabe to the pan with the sausage and cook until wilted, about 2 to 3 minutes. Season with lemon juice, lemon zest, crushed red pepper, salt and freshly ground pepper. Reduce the heat to low and keep warm.

Carefully drop the pasta into the boiling water and cook until al dente, about 2 to 3 minutes. Add the pasta to the broccoli rabe pan and toss to combine. To serve, divide the pasta between plates.

HERB FAZZOLETTI WITH TUNA AND CASTELVETRANO OLIVES

The fazzoletti, or "handkerchief pasta," named for its flattened, square shape, are beautiful in this dish, with the look of the pressed herbs or flowers between the sheets of dough.

SERVES 4–6

FAZZOLETTI

Egg Dough (page 19)

Herbs or edible flowers

TO FINISH

Olive oil

2 garlic cloves, minced

1 fennel bulb, thinly sliced, fronds reserved

1 (5-oz [142-g]) can tuna in olive oil

1 cup (180 g) Castelvetrano olives, pitted and chopped

1 lemon, juice and zest

Kosher salt

Freshly ground black pepper

Dust two sheet pans with semolina flour.

To make the pasta, roll out the dough until the sheet is just translucent (see page 17). Cut the rolled out sheets into 12-inch (30-cm) sections and cover the rest with plastic wrap. Lay the sheets on a dry work surface and place the herbs down the entire sheet, spaced apart. Place another pasta sheet on top and press down to seal. Pass the sheet again through the machine or roll by hand to seal in the herbs. Using a straight wheel cutter or a knife, cut the pasta sheets into 2-inch (5-cm) squares. Carefully place the fazzoletti on the semolina-dusted sheet pans, spaced apart.

Bring a large pot of water to a boil.

In a large sauté pan, over medium heat, add a drizzle of olive oil, garlic, fennel, tuna and olives. Carefully drop the pasta into the boiling water and cook until al dente, about 2 to 3 minutes. Add the pasta to the pan and season with lemon juice, lemon zest, salt and freshly ground black pepper.

To serve, divide the pasta between bowls. Garnish with fennel fronds.

SORPRESE WITH ROASTED BUTTERNUT SQUASH AND HAZELNUTS

The tiny, egg-shaped sorprese pasta in this dish and the nutty notes combine for an autumnal tasty treat.

SERVES 4–6

BUTTERNUT SQUASH

Olive oil

2 garlic cloves

1 butternut squash, peeled and cut into ½-inch (12-mm) cubes

Crushed red pepper, to taste

Kosher salt

Freshly ground black pepper

SORPRESE

Egg Dough (page 19)

TO FINISH

Olive oil

¼ cup (58 g) unsalted butter

Kosher salt

Freshly ground black pepper

¼ cup (43 g) hazelnuts, chopped and toasted

Parmigiano-Reggiano, for grating

Mint, torn

Preheat the oven to 350°F (177°C).

To make the roasted butternut squash, combine olive oil, garlic, cut squash, crushed red pepper, salt and freshly ground black pepper in a bowl. Place on a sheet pan and roast in the oven until tender, about 35 to 40 minutes. Set aside.

Dust two sheet pans with semolina flour.

To make the pasta, roll out the dough until the sheet is about ¹⁄₁₆-inch (1.6-mm) thick (see page 17). Cut the rolled-out sheets into 12-inch (30-cm) sections and cover the rest with plastic wrap. Lay the sheets on a dry work surface and, using a straight wheel cutter or a knife, cut the pasta sheets into 1-inch (2.5-cm) squares. To form the shape, hold the dough square in your hands, fold over the opposite corners and pinch together. Then with the free corners, fold over in the opposite direction and pinch together. The shape should resemble a piece of origami. Place the sorprese on the semolina dusted sheet pans, spaced apart.

Bring a large pot of salted water to a boil.

In a large sauté pan, over medium-high heat, add a drizzle of olive oil, butter and roasted squash and toss to combine. Carefully drop the pasta into the boiling water and cook until al dente, about 2 to 3 minutes. Add the cooked pasta to the sauté pan and season with salt and freshly ground black pepper.

To serve, divide the pasta between bowls. Garnish with chopped hazelnuts, grated Parmigiano-Reggiano and mint.

CHAPTER SIX

BAKED PASTA

Baked pastas are, essentially, the result of inspired creativity. In Renaissance Italy, baked pastas were often served at large palace banquets and are still associated with "special occasion" staples of the Italian (and American) table. When entertaining on a large scale, baked and sheeted pastas are still a go-to for many chefs. Often, one serving is a complete meal in itself—vegetables, cheese, meat and carbohydrates. As opposed to some of the more complicated dishes in the chapters featuring cut and stuffed pasta, the recipes in this section were born initially of necessity, often using up leftovers or tailoring a dish to a visiting guest, and therefore lack some of the hard-and-fast rules we often associate with Italian cooking. Of course, the recipes I've cultivated here are specific to my experience in the kitchen, so I urge you to make them first as written, and experiment once you've established a baseline for success.

In terms of technique, baked pastas require slightly more sauce than their unbaked counterparts since some of the sauce gets soaked up by the pasta and some evaporates in the oven. When distributing the sauce before baking, be sure each dish is well coated. Also, season as you go: a baked dish is difficult to season once assembled (like trying to add flour to a frosted cupcake). Just aim to make each component of the dish able to stand on its own. To prevent these dishes from becoming soggy in the oven and to achieve a browned top, bake the pasta uncovered, and be sure to let each dish rest before serving.

RATATOUILLE LASAGNA

This light spin on a traditional Italian layered lasagna dish is open to interpretation and to seasonal availability; try to get your hands on as many of the robust vegetable ingredients listed in the recipe, or substitute for whatever looks good at the farmers market.

SERVES 8–10

LASAGNA

Egg Dough (page 19)

TOMATO SAUCE

Extra-virgin olive oil

3 garlic cloves, chopped

1 cup (237 ml) red wine

2 (28-oz [794-g]) cans crushed tomatoes

1 bunch basil

Kosher salt

Freshly ground black pepper

FILLING

Olive oil

1 eggplant, peeled and diced small

1 green zucchini, diced small

1 summer squash, diced small

2 tomatoes, diced small

4 garlic cloves, sliced

1 red onion, thinly sliced

Kosher salt

Freshly ground black pepper

3 cups (390 g) shredded mozzarella

Preheat the oven to 350°F (177°C) and bring a large pot of salted water to a boil.

Dust two sheet pans with semolina flour. To make the pasta, roll out the dough until the sheet is about ⅟₁₆-inch (1.6-mm) thick (see page 17). Cut the rolled-out sheets into 12-inch (30-cm) sections and place them on sheet pans until you have about 20 sheets. Working in batches, drop the sheets into the boiling water and cook until just pliable, about 1 minute. Place on paper towels and pat dry.

To make the sauce, in a pot on medium heat, add the extra-virgin olive oil, garlic and sauté for about a minute or until translucent. Add the red wine and let it reduce by half. Then add the crushed tomatoes, basil and salt and pepper. Let it simmer on low for about 30 minutes.

To make the filling, in a large sauté pan over high heat, add a drizzle of olive oil, eggplant, zucchini, squash, tomatoes, garlic and red onion. Season with salt and freshly ground black pepper.

To assemble, place the sauce on the bottom of a 9 × 13-inch (22.9 × 33-cm) baking dish. Place the pasta sheets down, overlapping them slightly, covering the bottom of the dish. Add the ratatouille evenly over the pasta sheets and sprinkle mozzarella over the top. Add the next layer of pasta sheets in the opposite direction and repeat these layers until you reach the top or all of the filling has been used. Ladle some sauce evenly over the top sheet and sprinkle with some more mozzarella.

Place the lasagna in the oven and cook for about 45 minutes to 1 hour. Allow it to cool for about 10 minutes before cutting and serving.

EGGPLANT CANNELLONI

The vegetarian equivalent of short ribs in terms of comfort food, this supremely satisfying meatless baked pasta dish made with "large reed" pasta, or cannelloni, can often be made from things you already have in your well-stocked kitchen.

SERVES 6–8

CANNELLONI
Egg Dough (page 19)

TOMATO SAUCE
Olive oil

3 garlic cloves, chopped

1 cup (237 ml) red wine

2 (28-oz [794-g]) cans crushed tomatoes

1 bunch basil

Kosher salt

Freshly ground black pepper

FILLING
Olive oil

1 eggplant, peeled and diced small

4 garlic cloves, sliced

3 sprigs rosemary, chopped

4 cups (908 g) ricotta cheese

1 cup (130 g) shredded mozzarella

Kosher salt

Freshly ground black pepper

Preheat the oven to 350°F (177°C) and bring a large pot of salted water to a boil.

Dust two sheet pans with semolina flour. To make the pasta, roll out the dough until the sheet is about 1⁄16-inch (1.6-mm) thick (see page 17). Cut the rolled-out sheets into 6-inch (15-cm) sections and place them on the sheet pans until you have about 20 sheets. Working in batches, drop the sheets into the boiling water and cook until just pliable, about 1 minute. Place on paper towels and pat dry.

To make the sauce, in a pot on medium heat, add the olive oil and garlic and sauté for about a minute or until translucent. Add the red wine and let it reduce by half. Then add the crushed tomatoes, basil, salt and pepper. Let it simmer on low for about 30 minutes.

To make the filling, in a large sauté pan over high heat, add a drizzle of olive oil, eggplant, garlic and rosemary and cook until soft, about 4 to 5 minutes. Allow to cool and mix in a bowl with the ricotta and mozzarella. Season with salt and freshly ground black pepper.

To assemble, place the sauce on the bottom of a 9 × 13-inch (22.9 × 33-cm) baking dish. With the pasta sheet lengthwise, place about 3 tablespoons (45 g) of filling down at the edge closest to you. Carefully roll the pasta away from you, encasing the filling. Place the stuffed cannelloni in a single layer in the baking dish. Place some more sauce on top of the cannelloni and sprinkle with shredded mozzarella.

Place the cannelloni in the oven and cook for about 45 minutes.

SPINACH AND TALEGGIO ROTOLO

This "scroll" or "coiled" pasta has a crunchy component, and the mild Taleggio cheese makes this a great dish for sharing, potlucks, events involving (fancy) children, etc. It is also my personal, high-end alternative to baking for a neighbor.

SERVES 6–8

ROTOLO
Egg Dough (page 19)

SAUCE
Olive oil

3 garlic cloves, chopped

1 cup (237 ml) red wine

2 (28-oz [794-g]) cans crushed tomatoes

1 bunch basil

Kosher salt

Freshly ground black pepper

FILLING
Olive oil

2 lb (907 g) spinach

1 garlic clove, minced

Kosher salt

Freshly ground black pepper

8 oz (227 g) Taleggio cheese, grated

2 cups (454 g) sheep's milk ricotta

½ cup (90 g) grated Parmigiano-Reggiano

1 bunch basil, thinly sliced

TO FINISH
Parmigiano-Reggiano, for grating

Basil, torn

Preheat the oven to 350°F (177°C) and bring a large pot of salted water to a boil.

Dust two sheet pans with semolina flour. To make the pasta, roll out the dough until the sheet is about 1/16-inch (1.6-mm) thick (see page 17). Cut the rolled-out sheets into 6-inch (15-cm) sections and place them on the sheet pans until you have about 20 sheets. Working in batches, drop the sheets into the boiling water and cook until just pliable, about 1 minute. Place on paper towels and pat dry.

To make the sauce, in a pot on medium heat, add the extra-virgin olive oil and garlic and sauté for about a minute or until translucent. Add the red wine and let it reduce by half. Then add the crushed tomatoes, basil, salt and pepper. Let it simmer on low for about 30 minutes.

To make the filling, in a large sauté pan over medium heat, add a drizzle of olive oil, spinach and garlic. Cook until the spinach is wilted and season with salt and freshly ground black pepper. Allow it to cool. In a large bowl combine the spinach with the Taleggio, ricotta, grated Parmigiano-Reggiano and basil.

To assemble, place the sauce on the bottom of a 9 × 13-inch (22.9 × 33-cm) baking dish. With the pasta sheet lengthwise, place about 3 tablespoons (45 g) of filling down at the edge closest to you. Carefully roll the pasta away from you, encasing the filling. Then cut the rolls into 3-inch (7.5-cm) pieces. Place the rotolo, filling-side up, in a single layer in the baking dish. Place some more sauce over the top of the pasta and sprinkle with grated Parmigiano-Reggiano and basil.

Place the rotolo in the oven and cook for about 30 minutes. Garnish with some more fresh basil.

ESCAROLE AND SAUSAGE CANNELLONI

These resilient pasta tubes are a great counterpoint to the robust sausage and creamy ricotta; feel free to add more or less Parmigiano-Reggiano to taste, but be sure to balance with the creamy ricotta filling.

SERVES 6–8

CANNELLONI

Egg Dough (page 19)

CREAM SAUCE

3 tbsp (43 g) unsalted butter

3 garlic cloves, chopped

3 tbsp (24 g) flour

2 cups (472 ml) milk

¼ cup (45 g) grated Parmigiano-Reggiano

Kosher salt

Freshly ground black pepper

FILLING

Olive oil

8 oz (227 g) sweet Italian sausage, removed from casing

1 lb (454 g) broccoli rabe, chopped

2 garlic cloves, minced

Crushed red pepper, to taste

Kosher salt

Freshly ground black pepper

1 cup (227 g) ricotta

½ cup (90 g) grated Parmigiano-Reggiano

TO FINISH

Basil, torn

Preheat the oven to 350°F (177°C) and bring a large pot of salted water to a boil.

Dust two sheet pans with semolina flour. To make the pasta, roll out the dough until the sheet is about ¹⁄₁₆-inch (1.6-mm) thick (see page 17). Cut the rolled-out sheets into 6-inch (15-cm) sections and place them on the sheet pans until you have about 20 sheets. Working in batches, drop the sheets into the boiling water and cook until just pliable, about 1 minute. Place on paper towels and pat dry.

To make the cream sauce, in a pot on medium heat, add the butter, garlic and flour to make a roux. Cook for about 2 to 3 minutes, or until it has a nutty aroma. Then add the milk and Parmigiano-Reggiano and whisk well to combine. Season with salt and freshly ground black pepper.

To make the filling, in a large sauté pan, drizzle olive oil and brown the sausage. Then add the broccoli rabe and garlic. Cook until the broccoli rabe is wilted and season with crushed red pepper, salt and freshly ground black pepper. Allow it to cool. In a large bowl combine the sausage and broccoli rabe with the ricotta and grated Parmigiano-Reggiano.

To assemble, place the sauce on the bottom of a 9 × 13-inch (22.9 × 33-cm) baking dish. With the pasta sheet lengthwise, place about 3 tablespoons (45 g) of filling down at the edge closest to you. Carefully roll the pasta away from you, encasing the filling. Place the stuffed cannelloni in a single layer in the baking dish. Place some more sauce over the top of the cannelloni and sprinkle with grated Parmigiano-Reggiano.

Place the cannelloni in the oven and cook for about 45 minutes. Garnish with basil.

GRANDMA ROSIE'S TIMBALLO

This recipe is a variation on my Grandma Rosie's ricotta pie. Wrapping the pie mixture in delicate sheets of pasta and baking it creates a crunchy outer layer that never got included in the original recipe. Feel free to also layer the pasta sheathes like lasagna—either way, this dish is one of my favorites to sit around the table enjoying with my family both on holidays and on any given Thursday. I hope you enjoy it with your family as I do.

SERVES 6–8

TIMBALLO
Egg Dough (page 19)

FILLING
3 eggs

1 cup (180 g) grated Parmigiano-Reggiano

1 bunch Italian flat-leaf parsley, chopped

3 cups (681 g) ricotta cheese

1 cup (227 g) hot or sweet soppressata, chopped

TO FINISH
1 egg, beaten

Preheat the oven to 350°F (177°C) and bring a large pot of salted water to a boil.

Dust two sheet pans with semolina flour. To make the pasta, roll out the dough until the sheet is about 1⁄16-inch (1.6-mm) thick (see page 17). Cut the rolled-out sheets into 12-inch (30-cm) sections and place them on the sheet pans until you have about 10 sheets. Working in batches, drop the sheets into the boiling water and cook until just pliable, about 1 minute. Place on paper towels and pat dry. In a lightly oiled 9-inch (22.9-cm) springform pan, begin to lay the cooked sheets of pasta down, overlapping one another and ensuring the pan is fully covered. Pasta should be long enough to hang over the sides of the pan.

In a large mixing bowl, combine the eggs, grated Parmigiano-Reggiano, parsley, ricotta and soppressata. Place the filling in the pasta-lined pan and begin to cover the filling piece by piece with the hanging sheets of pasta. Brush the top of the pasta with egg wash and place in the oven. Cook for 1 hour. Allow it to cool for about 10 minutes before cutting and serving.

SOURCES

FANTES KITCHEN SHOP
fantes.com

LUNDY WAY APRONS
lundyway.com

ANDREW BOSWELL CERAMICS
sonofapotter.com

FATTO IN AMERICA
artisanalpastatools.com

CALANDRA'S CHEESE
Calandrascheese.com

ARTHUR AVE MARKET
arthuravenuebronx.com

RANDAZZO'S SEAFOOD

ABOUT THE AUTHOR

Nicole Karr is a professional chef and native New Yorker. She has appeared on the Food Network and has worked in restaurants in Italy, Maine and all around New York City. If it involves food, Nicole has done it. Her career has taken her from teaching cooking classes to catering to private chef work and food styling for top brands. Nicole has gone back to her restaurant roots and currently works as a pastaia in NYC. Her love of pasta can be matched only by her love for her pup, Peanut.

FIND HER AT:
Instagram: chefnk

chefnicolekarr.com

ACKNOWLEDGMENTS

In an effort not to offend anyone (almost impossible with Italians), I want to thank my entire family. It's the memories I had with all of you growing up that really inspired me to become a chef and write this book.

My parents, Peter and Theresa. I know I've never done anything the practical or normal way, but it seemed to have all worked out. Thank you for always supporting me, through some pretty dark times and all of my great accomplishments. I love you.

Crystal and Thomas, you're lucky to have a sister like me. Love you and thanks for always telling me when you thought something I made was bad.

Most importantly, Christina Sico, my amazing photographer and cousin. I know I'm not the easiest person to work with and I'm sure there were multiple instances where you wanted to strangle me, but your professionalism and patience working with me on this book was greatly appreciated.

Chef Eric LeVine, for sharing your years of knowledge and experience. Your endless support and encouragement throughout this whole book process and on a personal level as well has been extremely invaluable.

Jamie Mattocks and Lulu Chutz, for helping bring my ideas to light when I just needed that extra hand.

Thanks to Luca Donofrio, Ashley Holt, Patricia Vega, Christian Petroni, Russell Jackson, Scott Conant, Jenn Louis and Michele Regussis for the kind words and setting the bar for work ethic and passion in this industry.

Sincere gratitude to everyone who helped me make this book possible. Who edited, proofread, designed and read this over and over again to ensure it was the best it could be. Thank you Page Street, Marissa Giambelluca, Meg Baskis, Laura Gallant, William Kiester and anyone else who made this into a reality.

INDEX

00 flour
  Beet Gnocchi with Sheep's Milk Ricotta and Sage, 80
  Cecamariti with Figs, Pancetta and Brussels Sprouts, 42
  Egg Dough, 19
  Egg Yolk Gnudi with Truffles, 72
  introduction to, 14
  Mint Corzetti with Lamb Sausage and Broccoli Rabe, 168
  Pizzoccheri with Swiss Chard, Fingerlings and Grana Padana, 155
  Pumpkin Gnocchi with Pancetta and Swiss Chard Pesto, 75
  Ramp Gnudi and Grana Padano, 79
  Ravioli Dough, 20
  Ricotta Cavatelli with Mussels, 32
  Roasted Potato Gnocchi with Robiola, Artichokes and Capers, 85–86
  Saffron Gnocchi with Butter Poached Lobster and Tarragon, 83–84
  Semolina Dough, 21
  Sweet Potato Gnocchi with Pecans and Prosciutto, 76

agnolotti, in Veal Agnolotti with Mustard Greens and Pecorino, 105–106
all-purpose flour, in Capunti with Crispy Calamari, Kale and Burrata, 36–38
almonds, in Culurgiones with Brown Butter and Almonds, 132
anchovies
  Fusilli with Roasted Cauliflower and Anchovies, 25–26
  Tagliarini with Cerignola Olives and Lemon, 156
Anolini in Brodo, 111
apples
  Pork and Parsnip Tortelli with Apples and Walnuts, 126–128
  Sunchoke Cappelletti with Kale and Apples, 121
artichokes
  Artichoke Casonsei with Hazelnuts and Goat's Milk Ricotta, 125
  Casarecce with Crispy Artichokes, Lemon and Scamorza, 63–64
  Herb Garganelli with Artichokes and Meyer Lemon, 163
  Roasted Potato Gnocchi with Robiola, Artichokes and Capers, 85–86
asparagus, in Tagliatelle Primavera, 142

baccala, in Roasted Garlic Fettuccine with Razor Clams and Baccala, 136–138
beef, ground
  Anolini in Brodo, 111
  Orecchiette and Meatballs, 51–53
beef stock
  Espresso Braised Short Rib and Celery Root Ravioli, 115
  Malloreddus with Juniper Berry Braised Venison, 39–41
  Radicchio and Taleggio Triangoli with Pork Cheek Ragu, 116–119
beets
  Beet and Rose Scarpinocc with Poppy Seeds, 129–131
  Beet Gnocchi with Sheep's Milk Ricotta and Sage, 80
bench scrapers, 12
Black Pepper Trofie with Clams, Fennel and Sausage, 45–46
boiling, 18
brasciole, in Maccheroni di Busa with Brasciole and Pomodoro Sauce, 54–56
briganti, in Cappellacci dei Briganti with Eggplant Caponata, 164
broccoli
  Escarole and Sausage Cannelloni, 183
  Mint Corzetti with Lamb Sausage and Broccoli Rabe, 168
brussels sprouts, in Cecamariti with Figs, Pancetta and Brussels Sprouts, 42
buckwheat flour, in Pizzoccheri with Swiss Chard, Fingerlings and Grana Padana, 155
burrata, in Capunti with Crispy Calamari, Kale and Burrata, 36–38
butternut squash
  Butternut Squash and Roasted Pear Cappellacci with Sage, 101–102
  Sorprese with Roasted Butternut Squash and Hazelnuts, 172

calamari, in Capunti with Crispy Calamari, Kale and Burrata, 36–38
cannelloni
  Eggplant Cannelloni, 179
  Escarole and Sausage Cannelloni, 183
capers
  Cappellacci dei Briganti with Eggplant Caponata, 164
  Roasted Potato Gnocchi with Robiola, Artichokes and Capers, 85–86

Tagliarini with Cerignola Olives and Lemon, 156
cappellacci
  Butternut Squash and Roasted Pear Cappellacci with Sage, 101–102
  Cappellacci dei Briganti with Eggplant Caponata, 164
cappelletti, in Sunchoke Cappelletti with Kale and Apples, 121
Capunti with Crispy Calamari, Kale and Burrata, 36–38
caramelle, in Prosciutto Caramelle with Gorgonzola Fonduta, 107–108
carrots
  Anolini in Brodo, 111
  Chestnut Stracci with Braised Pork Ribs and Pears, 160
  Ciciones with Lentil Stew, 60
  Cocoa Mafaldine with Quail and Walnuts, 151
  Espresso Braised Short Rib and Celery Root Ravioli, 115
  Malloreddus with Juniper Berry Braised Venison, 39–41
  Pappardelle with Wild Mushroom Bolognese, 147–148
  Radicchio and Taleggio Triangoli with Pork Cheek Ragu, 116–119
Casarecce with Crispy Artichokes, Lemon and Scamorza, 63–64
casonsei, in Artichoke Casonsei with Hazelnuts and Goat's Milk Ricotta, 125
cauliflower, in Fusilli with Roasted Cauliflower and Anchovies, 25–26
cavarola boards, 12
cavatelli
  Ricotta Cavatelli with Mussels, 32
  Whole Wheat Cavatelli with Mushrooms and Goat Cheese Crema, 27–28
Cecamariti with Figs, Pancetta and Brussels Sprouts, 42
celery
  Anolini in Brodo, 111
  Chestnut Stracci with Braised Pork Ribs and Pears, 160
  Ciciones with Lentil Stew, 60
  Cocoa Mafaldine with Quail and Walnuts, 151
  Espresso Braised Short Rib and Celery Root Ravioli, 115
  Malloreddus with Juniper Berry Braised Venison, 39–41
  Pappardelle with Wild Mushroom Bolognese, 147–148
  Radicchio and Taleggio Triangoli with Pork Cheek Ragu, 116–119

chestnut flour
  Chestnut Stracci with Braised Pork Ribs and Pears, 160
  Roasted Potato Gnocchi with Robiola, Artichokes and Capers, 85–86
chicken stock
  Artichoke Casonsei with Hazelnuts and Goat's Milk Ricotta, 125
  Chestnut Stracci with Braised Pork Ribs and Pears, 160
  Cocoa Mafaldine with Quail and Walnuts, 151
  Herb Garganelli with Artichokes and Meyer Lemon, 163
  Roasted Potato Gnocchi with Robiola, Artichokes and Capers, 85–86
chickpea flour, in Chickpea Gnudi with Heirloom Tomatoes, 90
chickpeas, in Ink Farfalle with Octopus, Calabrian Chiles and Chickpeas, 167
chile peppers
  Farfalle with Roasted Tomatoes and Chile, 139–141
  Ink Farfalle with Octopus, Calabrian Chiles and Chickpeas, 167
chitarra, 12
Ciciones with Lentil Stew, 60
clams
  Black Pepper Trofie with Clams, Fennel and Sausage, 45–46
  Roasted Garlic Fettuccine with Razor Clams and Baccala, 136–138
  Cocoa Mafaldine with Quail and Walnuts, 151
corn
  Frascatelli with Sweet Corn Carbonara, 31
cornmeal
  Capunti with Crispy Calamari, Kale and Burrata, 36–38
  Polenta Raviolo with Guanciale and Wild Mushrooms, 96
corzetti
  corzetti stamps, 12
  Mint Corzetti with Lamb Sausage and Broccoli Rabe, 168
crabmeat, in Strozzapreti with Green Tomatoes and Crab, 69
Crispy Lemon Gnocchi with Sweet Peas and Scallops, 89
Culurgiones with Brown Butter and Almonds, 132

dopio zero (00) flour
    Beet Gnocchi with Sheep's Milk Ricotta and Sage, 80
    Cecamariti with Figs, Pancetta and Brussels Sprouts, 42
    Egg Dough, 19
    Egg Yolk Gnudi with Truffles, 72
    introduction to, 14
    Mint Corzetti with Lamb Sausage and Broccoli Rabe, 168
    Pizzoccheri with Swiss Chard, Fingerlings and Grana Padana, 155
    Pumpkin Gnocchi with Pancetta and Swiss Chard Pesto, 75
    Ramp Gnudi and Grana Padano, 79
    Ravioli Dough, 20
    Ricotta Cavatelli with Mussels, 32
    Roasted Potato Gnocchi with Robiola, Artichokes and Capers, 85–86
    Saffron Gnocchi with Butter Poached Lobster and Tarragon, 83–84
    Semolina Dough, 21
    Sweet Potato Gnocchi with Pecans and Prosciutto, 76

dough
    Egg Dough, 19
    Extruded Dough, 21
    flour, 13–14
    kneading, 17
    measuring, 15
    mixing, 15
    Ravioli Dough, 20
    resting, 17
    rolling, 17
    salt, 15
    Semolina Dough, 21
    shaping, 17–18
    water, 14

drying racks, 12

Egg Dough, 19
    Cappellacci dei Briganti with Eggplant Caponata, 164
    Chestnut Stracci with Braised Pork Ribs and Pears, 160
    Cocoa Mafaldine with Quail and Walnuts, 151
    Eggplant Cannelloni, 179
    Escarole and Sausage Cannelloni, 183
    Farfalle with Roasted Tomatoes and Chile, 139–141
    Grandma Rosie's Timballo, 184
    Herb Fazzoletti with Tuna and Castelvetrano Olives, 171
    Herb Fettuccine with Mussels and Speck, 152

    Herb Garganelli with Artichokes and Meyer Lemon, 163
    Ink Farfalle with Octopus, Calabrian Chiles and Chickpeas, 167
    Ink Spaghetti alla Chitarra with Cured Yolk and Poached Egg, 145–146
    Pappardelle with Wild Mushroom Bolognese, 147–148
    Ratatouille Lasagna, 176
    Roasted Garlic Fettuccine with Razor Clams and Baccala, 136–138
    Sorprese with Roasted Butternut Squash and Hazelnuts, 172
    Spaghetti Cacio e Pepe, 159
    Spinach and Taleggio Rotolo, 180
    Tagliarini with Cerignola Olives and Lemon, 156
    Tagliatelle Primavera, 142

eggplant
    Cappellacci dei Briganti with Eggplant Caponata, 164
    Eggplant Cannelloni, 179
    Eggplant Mezzaluna with Tomato Confit and Pesto, 99–100
    Ratatouille Lasagna, 176

eggs, introduction to, 14
Egg Yolk Gnudi with Truffles, 72
equipment, 12–13
Escarole and Sausage Cannelloni, 183
Espresso Braised Short Rib and Celery Root Ravioli, 115
Extruded Dough, 21

Faggotini with Dill, Shrimp and Zucchini, 122
farfalle
    Farfalle with Roasted Tomatoes and Chile, 139–141
    Ink Farfalle with Octopus, Calabrian Chiles and Chickpeas, 167
fava beans, in Gnocchetti with Fava Beans, Shrimp and Pistachio Pesto, 57–59
fazzoletti, in Herb Fazzoletti with Tuna and Castelvetrano Olives, 171
fennel
    Black Pepper Trofie with Clams, Fennel and Sausage, 45–46
    Herb Fazzoletti with Tuna and Castelvetrano Olives, 171
    Ink Farfalle with Octopus, Calabrian Chiles and Chickpeas, 167
    Ricotta Cavatelli with Mussels, 32
    Roasted Garlic Fettuccine with Razor Clams and Baccala, 136–138
    Whole Wheat Cavatelli with Mushrooms and Goat Cheese Crema, 27–28

fettuccine
    Herb Fettuccine with Mussels and Speck, 152
    Roasted Garlic Fettuccine with Razor Clams and Baccala, 136–138
figs, in Cecamariti with Figs, Pancetta and Brussels Sprouts, 42
Frascatelli with Sweet Corn Carbonara, 31
Fusilli with Roasted Cauliflower and Anchovies, 25–26

garganelli
    garganelli boards, 12
    Herb Garganelli with Artichokes and Meyer Lemon, 163
garlic
    Anolini in Brodo, 111
    Artichoke Casonsei with Hazelnuts and Goat's Milk Ricotta, 125
    Black Pepper Trofie with Clams, Fennel and Sausage, 45–46
    Cappellacci dei Briganti with Eggplant Caponata, 164
    Capunti with Crispy Calamari, Kale and Burrata, 36–38
    Cecamariti with Figs, Pancetta and Brussels Sprouts, 42
    Chestnut Stracci with Braised Pork Ribs and Pears, 160
    Chickpea Gnudi with Heirloom Tomatoes, 90
    Ciciones with Lentil Stew, 60
    Cocoa Mafaldine with Quail and Walnuts, 151
    Eggplant Cannelloni, 179
    Eggplant Mezzaluna with Tomato Confit and Pesto, 99–100
    Escarole and Sausage Cannelloni, 183
    Espresso Braised Short Rib and Celery Root Ravioli, 115
    Farfalle with Roasted Tomatoes and Chile, 139–141
    Fusilli with Roasted Cauliflower and Anchovies, 25–26
    Gnocchetti with Fava Beans, Shrimp and Pistachio Pesto, 57–59
    Herb Fazzoletti with Tuna and Castelvetrano Olives, 171
    Herb Fettuccine with Mussels and Speck, 152
    Herb Garganelli with Artichokes and Meyer Lemon, 163
    Ink Farfalle with Octopus, Calabrian Chiles and Chickpeas, 167
    Lorighittas with Heirloom Tomatoes, 'Nduja and Oil-Cured Olives, 47–48
    Maccheroni di Busa with Brasciole and Pomodoro Sauce, 54–56

Malloreddus with Juniper Berry Braised Venison, 39–41
Mezzi Paccheri with Peas and Onions, 65–66
Mint Corzetti with Lamb Sausage and Broccoli Rabe, 168
Orecchiette and Meatballs, 51–53
Pappardelle with Wild Mushroom Bolognese, 147–148
Pizzoccheri with Swiss Chard, Fingerlings and Grana Padana, 155
Pork and Parsnip Tortelli with Apples and Walnuts, 126–128
Pumpkin Gnocchi with Pancetta and Swiss Chard Pesto, 75
Radicchio and Taleggio Triangoli with Pork Cheek Ragu, 116–119
Ratatouille Lasagna, 176
Ricotta Cavatelli with Mussels, 32
Roasted Garlic Fettuccine with Razor Clams and Baccala, 136–138
Roasted Potato Gnocchi with Robiola, Artichokes and Capers, 85–86
Saffron Gnocchi with Butter Poached Lobster and Tarragon, 83–84
Sorprese with Roasted Butternut Squash and Hazelnuts, 172
Spinach and Taleggio Rotolo, 180
Strozzapreti with Green Tomatoes and Crab, 69
Sunchoke Cappelletti with Kale and Apples, 121
Tagliarini with Cerignola Olives and Lemon, 156
Tagliatelle Primavera, 142
Veal Agnolotti with Mustard Greens and Pecorino, 105–106
ginger, in Pumpkin Gnocchi with Pancetta and Swiss Chard Pesto, 75
Gnocchetti with Fava Beans, Shrimp and Pistachio Pesto, 57–59
gnocchi
    Beet Gnocchi with Sheep's Milk Ricotta and Sage, 80
    Crispy Lemon Gnocchi with Sweet Peas and Scallops, 89
    gnocchi boards, 12
    Gnocchi Verdi with Provolone Fonduta, 93
    Pumpkin Gnocchi with Pancetta and Swiss Chard Pesto, 75
    Roasted Potato Gnocchi with Robiola, Artichokes and Capers, 85–86
    Saffron Gnocchi with Butter Poached Lobster and Tarragon, 83–84
    Sweet Potato Gnocchi with Pecans and Prosciutto, 76

gnudi

    Chickpea Gnudi with Heirloom Tomatoes, 90

    Egg Yolk Gnudi with Truffles, 72

    Ramp Gnudi and Grana Padano, 79

goat cheese, in Whole Wheat Cavatelli with Mushrooms and Goat Cheese Crema, 27–28

Gorgonzola cheese, in Prosciutto Caramelle with Gorgonzola Fonduta, 107–108

Grana Padano cheese

    Pizzoccheri with Swiss Chard, Fingerlings and Grana Padana, 155

    Ramp Gnudi and Grana Padano, 79

Grandma Rosie's Timballo, 184

green tomatoes, in Strozzapreti with Green Tomatoes and Crab, 69

guanciale

    Crispy Lemon Gnocchi with Sweet Peas and Scallops, 89

    Pici with Black Pepper, Pecorino and Guanciale, 35

    Polenta Raviolo with Guanciale and Wild Mushrooms, 96

hazelnuts

    Artichoke Casonsei with Hazelnuts and Goat's Milk Ricotta, 125

    Cecamariti with Figs, Pancetta and Brussels Sprouts, 42

    Sorprese with Roasted Butternut Squash and Hazelnuts, 172

Herb Fazzoletti with Tuna and Castelvetrano Olives, 171

Herb Fettuccine with Mussels and Speck, 152

Herb Garganelli with Artichokes and Meyer Lemon, 163

Ink Farfalle with Octopus, Calabrian Chiles and Chickpeas, 167

Ink Spaghetti alla Chitarra with Cured Yolk and Poached Egg, 145–146

Italian sausage

    Black Pepper Trofie with Clams, Fennel and Sausage, 45–46

    Escarole and Sausage Cannelloni, 183

juniper berries, in Malloreddus with Juniper Berry Braised Venison, 39–41

kale

    Capunti with Crispy Calamari, Kale and Burrata, 36–38

    Sunchoke Cappelletti with Kale and Apples, 121

lamb sausage, in Mint Corzetti with Lamb Sausage and Broccoli Rabe, 168

lardo, in Frascatelli with Sweet Corn Carbonara, 31

lasagna, in Ratatouille Lasagna, 176

lentils, in Ciciones with Lentil Stew, 60

lobster, in Saffron Gnocchi with Butter Poached Lobster and Tarragon, 83–84

Lorighittas with Heirloom Tomatoes, 'Nduja and Oil-Cured Olives, 47–48

Maccheroni di Busa with Brasciole and Pomodoro Sauce, 54–56

mafaldine, in Cocoa Mafaldine with Quail and Walnuts, 151

Malloreddus with Juniper Berry Braised Venison, 39–41

mascarpone

    Beet and Rose Scarpinocc with Poppy Seeds, 129–131

    Sweet Pea Raviolini with Mascarpone and Mint, 112

mezzaluna, in Eggplant Mezzaluna with Tomato Confit and Pesto, 99–100

Mezzi Paccheri with Peas and Onions, 65–66

Mint Corzetti with Lamb Sausage and Broccoli Rabe, 168

mozzarella cheese

    Eggplant Cannelloni, 179

    Eggplant Mezzaluna with Tomato Confit and Pesto, 99–100

    Ratatouille Lasagna, 176

mushrooms

    Pappardelle with Wild Mushroom Bolognese, 147–148

    Polenta Raviolo with Guanciale and Wild Mushrooms, 96

    Whole Wheat Cavatelli with Mushrooms and Goat Cheese Crema, 27–28

mussels

    Herb Fettuccine with Mussels and Speck, 152

    Ricotta Cavatelli with Mussels, 32

mustard greens, in Veal Agnolotti with Mustard Greens and Pecorino, 105–106

'nduja, in Lorighittas with Heirloom Tomatoes, 'Nduja and Oil-Cured Olives, 47–48

octopus, in Ink Farfalle with Octopus, Calabrian Chiles and Chickpeas, 167

olives

    Herb Fazzoletti with Tuna and Castelvetrano Olives, 171

    Lorighittas with Heirloom Tomatoes, 'Nduja and Oil-Cured Olives,

47–48

    Tagliarini with Cerignola Olives and Lemon, 156

onions

    Anolini in Brodo, 111

    Artichoke Casonsei with Hazelnuts and Goat's Milk Ricotta, 125

    Cappellacci dei Briganti with Eggplant Caponata, 164

    Chestnut Stracci with Braised Pork Ribs and Pears, 160

    Ciciones with Lentil Stew, 60

    Cocoa Mafaldine with Quail and Walnuts, 151

    Eggplant Mezzaluna with Tomato Confit and Pesto, 99–100

    Espresso Braised Short Rib and Celery Root Ravioli, 115

    Herb Garganelli with Artichokes and Meyer Lemon, 163

    Ink Farfalle with Octopus, Calabrian Chiles and Chickpeas, 167

    Maccheroni di Busa with Brasciole and Pomodoro Sauce, 54–56

    Malloreddus with Juniper Berry Braised Venison, 39–41

    Mezzi Paccheri with Peas and Onions, 65–66

    Pappardelle with Wild Mushroom Bolognese, 147–148

    Radicchio and Taleggio Triangoli with Pork Cheek Ragu, 116–119

    Ratatouille Lasagna, 176

    Roasted Garlic Fettuccine with Razor Clams and Baccala, 136–138

    Roasted Potato Gnocchi with Robiola, Artichokes and Capers, 85–86

    Tagliatelle Primavera, 142

Orecchiette and Meatballs, 51–53

pancetta

    Cecamariti with Figs, Pancetta and Brussels Sprouts, 42

    Pumpkin Gnocchi with Pancetta and Swiss Chard Pesto, 75

Pappardelle with Wild Mushroom Bolognese, 147–148

Parmigiano-Reggiano cheese

    Anolini in Brodo, 111

    Beet Gnocchi with Sheep's Milk Ricotta and Sage, 80

    Butternut Squash and Roasted Pear Cappellacci with Sage, 101–102

    Cappellacci dei Briganti with Eggplant Caponata, 164

    Chestnut Stracci with Braised Pork Ribs and Pears, 160

    Eggplant Mezzaluna with Tomato Confit and Pesto, 99–100

Egg Yolk Gnudi with Truffles, 72

Escarole and Sausage Cannelloni, 183

Faggotini with Dill, Shrimp and Zucchini, 122

Frascatelli with Sweet Corn Carbonara, 31

Fusilli with Roasted Cauliflower and Anchovies, 25–26

Grandma Rosie's Timballo, 184

Maccheroni di Busa with Brasciole and Pomodoro Sauce, 54–56

Mezzi Paccheri with Peas and Onions, 65–66

Orecchiette and Meatballs, 51–53

Pappardelle with Wild Mushroom Bolognese, 147–148

Polenta Raviolo with Guanciale and Wild Mushrooms, 96

Roasted Garlic Fettuccine with Razor Clams and Baccala, 136–138

Sorprese with Roasted Butternut Squash and Hazelnuts, 172

Spinach and Taleggio Rotolo, 180

Sweet Pea Raviolini with Mascarpone and Mint, 112

Sweet Potato Gnocchi with Pecans and Prosciutto, 76

Tagliarini with Cerignola Olives and Lemon, 156

Tagliatelle Primavera, 142

parsnips, in Pork and Parsnip Tortelli with Apples and Walnuts, 126–128

pasta extruders, 12

pasta machines, 12

pastry brushes, 13

pastry wheels, 12

pears

    Butternut Squash and Roasted Pear Cappellacci with Sage, 101–102

    Chestnut Stracci with Braised Pork Ribs and Pears, 160

peas

    Crispy Lemon Gnocchi with Sweet Peas and Scallops, 89

    Mezzi Paccheri with Peas and Onions, 65–66

    Sweet Pea Raviolini with Mascarpone and Mint, 112

pecans, in Sweet Potato Gnocchi with Pecans and Prosciutto, 76

Pecorino Romano cheese

    Chickpea Gnudi with Heirloom Tomatoes, 90

    Culurgiones with Brown Butter and Almonds, 132

    Farfalle with Roasted Tomatoes and Chile, 139–141

    Gnocchetti with Fava Beans, Shrimp and Pistachio Pesto, 57–59

Herb Garganelli with Artichokes and Meyer Lemon, 163

Pici with Black Pepper, Pecorino and Guanciale, 35

Pork and Parsnip Tortelli with Apples and Walnuts, 126–128

Pumpkin Gnocchi with Pancetta and Swiss Chard Pesto, 75

Spaghetti Cacio e Pepe, 159

Veal Agnolotti with Mustard Greens and Pecorino, 105–106

Pici with Black Pepper, Pecorino and Guanciale, 35

pignoli nuts

  Cappellacci dei Briganti with Eggplant Caponata, 164

  Eggplant Mezzaluna with Tomato Confit and Pesto, 99–100

  Pumpkin Gnocchi with Pancetta and Swiss Chard Pesto, 75

piping bags, 13

pistachios, in Gnocchetti with Fava Beans, Shrimp and Pistachio Pesto, 57–59

Pizzoccheri with Swiss Chard, Fingerlings and Grana Padana, 155

Polenta Raviolo with Guanciale and Wild Mushrooms, 96

poppy seeds, in Beet and Rose Scarpinocc with Poppy Seeds, 129–131

Pork and Parsnip Tortelli with Apples and Walnuts, 126–128

pork cheek, in Radicchio and Taleggio Triangoli with Pork Cheek Ragu, 116–119

pork, ground

  Orecchiette and Meatballs, 51–53

  Pork and Parsnip Tortelli with Apples and Walnuts, 126–128

pork ribs, in Chestnut Stracci with Braised Pork Ribs and Pears, 160

potatoes

  Crispy Lemon Gnocchi with Sweet Peas and Scallops, 89

  Culurgiones with Brown Butter and Almonds, 132

  Gnocchi Verdi with Provolone Fonduta, 93

  Pizzoccheri with Swiss Chard, Fingerlings and Grana Padana, 155

  potato ricers, 13

  Roasted Potato Gnocchi with Robiola, Artichokes and Capers, 85–86

  Saffron Gnocchi with Butter Poached Lobster and Tarragon, 83–84

prosciutto

  Prosciutto Caramelle with Gorgonzola Fonduta, 107–108

  Sweet Potato Gnocchi with Pecans and Prosciutto, 76

provolone cheese, in Gnocchi Verdi with Provolone Fonduta, 93

Pumpkin Gnocchi with Pancetta and Swiss Chard Pesto, 75

quail, in Cocoa Mafaldine with Quail and Walnuts, 151

radicchio

  Prosciutto Caramelle with Gorgonzola Fonduta, 107–108

  Radicchio and Taleggio Triangoli with Pork Cheek Ragu, 116–119

Ramp Gnudi and Grana Padano, 79

Ratatouille Lasagna, 176

ravioli

  Espresso Braised Short Rib and Celery Root Ravioli, 115

  ravioli stamps, 13

Ravioli Dough, 20

  Anolini in Brodo, 111

  Artichoke Casonsei with Hazelnuts and Goat's Milk Ricotta, 125

  Beet and Rose Scarpinocc with Poppy Seeds, 129–131

  Butternut Squash and Roasted Pear Cappellacci with Sage, 101–102

  Eggplant Mezzaluna with Tomato Confit and Pesto, 99–100

  Espresso Braised Short Rib and Celery Root Ravioli, 115

  Faggotini with Dill, Shrimp and Zucchini, 122

  Polenta Raviolo with Guanciale and Wild Mushrooms, 96

  Pork and Parsnip Tortelli with Apples and Walnuts, 126–128

  Prosciutto Caramelle with Gorgonzola Fonduta, 107–108

  Radicchio and Taleggio Triangoli with Pork Cheek Ragu, 116–119

  Sunchoke Cappelletti with Kale and Apples, 121

  Sweet Pea Raviolini with Mascarpone and Mint, 112

  Veal Agnolotti with Mustard Greens and Pecorino, 105–106

raviolini, in Sweet Pea Raviolini with Mascarpone and Mint, 112

raviolo, in Polenta Raviolo with Guanciale and Wild Mushrooms, 96

ribs

  Chestnut Stracci with Braised Pork Ribs and Pears, 160

  Espresso Braised Short Rib and Celery Root Ravioli, 115

ricotta cheese

  Artichoke Casonsei with Hazelnuts and Goat's Milk Ricotta, 125

  Beet and Rose Scarpinocc with Poppy Seeds, 129–131

Beet Gnocchi with Sheep's Milk Ricotta and Sage, 80

Chickpea Gnudi with Heirloom Tomatoes, 90

Eggplant Cannelloni, 179

Egg Yolk Gnudi with Truffles, 72

Escarole and Sausage Cannelloni, 183

Faggotini with Dill, Shrimp and Zucchini, 122

Gnocchi Verdi with Provolone Fonduta, 93

Grandma Rosie's Timballo, 184

Polenta Raviolo with Guanciale and Wild Mushrooms, 96

Prosciutto Caramelle with Gorgonzola Fonduta, 107–108

Pumpkin Gnocchi with Pancetta and Swiss Chard Pesto, 75

Ramp Gnudi and Grana Padano, 79

Ricotta Cavatelli with Mussels, 32

Roasted Potato Gnocchi with Robiola, Artichokes and Capers, 85–86

Saffron Gnocchi with Butter Poached Lobster and Tarragon, 83–84

Spinach and Taleggio Rotolo, 180

Sunchoke Cappelletti with Kale and Apples, 121

Sweet Potato Gnocchi with Pecans and Prosciutto, 76

Roasted Garlic Fettuccine with Razor Clams and Baccala, 136–138

Roasted Potato Gnocchi with Robiola, Artichokes and Capers, 85, 85–86

robiola cheese, in Roasted Potato Gnocchi with Robiola, Artichokes and Capers, 85–86

rolling pins, 13

rotolo, in Spinach and Taleggio Rotolo, 180

Saffron Gnocchi with Butter Poached Lobster and Tarragon, 83–84

salt, introduction to, 15

sausage

  Black Pepper Trofie with Clams, Fennel and Sausage, 45–46

  Escarole and Sausage Cannelloni, 183

  Mint Corzetti with Lamb Sausage and Broccoli Rabe, 168

scales, 12

scallops, in Crispy Lemon Gnocchi with Sweet Peas and Scallops, 89

scamorza, in Casarecce with Crispy Artichokes, Lemon and Scamorza, 63–64

scarpinocc, in Beet and Rose Scarpinocc with Poppy Seeds, 129–131

scoops, 13

Semolina Dough, 21

  Black Pepper Trofie with Clams, Fennel and Sausage, 45–46

  Capunti with Crispy Calamari, Kale and Burrata, 36–38

  Casarecce with Crispy Artichokes, Lemon and Scamorza, 63–64

  Ciciones with Lentil Stew, 60

  Culurgiones with Brown Butter and Almonds, 132

  Fusilli with Roasted Cauliflower and Anchovies, 25–26

  Gnocchetti with Fava Beans, Shrimp and Pistachio Pesto, 57–59

  Lorighittas with Heirloom Tomatoes, 'Nduja and Oil-Cured Olives, 47–48

  Maccheroni di Busa with Brasciole and Pomodoro Sauce, 54–56

  Malloreddus with Juniper Berry Braised Venison, 39–41

  Mezzi Paccheri with Peas and Onions, 65–66

  Orecchiette and Meatballs, 51–53

  Pici with Black Pepper, Pecorino and Guanciale, 35

  Strozzapreti with Green Tomatoes and Crab, 69

  Whole Wheat Cavatelli with Mushrooms and Goat Cheese Crema, 27–28

semolina flour

  Capunti with Crispy Calamari, Kale and Burrata, 36–38

  Chickpea Gnudi with Heirloom Tomatoes, 90

  Crispy Lemon Gnocchi with Sweet Peas and Scallops, 89

  Extruded Dough, 21

  Frascatelli with Sweet Corn Carbonara, 31

  Gnocchi Verdi with Provolone Fonduta, 93

  introduction to, 13

  Semolina Dough, 21

  Whole Wheat Cavatelli with Mushrooms and Goat Cheese Crema, 27–28

shallots

  Black Pepper Trofie with Clams, Fennel and Sausage, 45–46

  Ricotta Cavatelli with Mussels, 32

short ribs, in Espresso Braised Short Rib and Celery Root Ravioli, 115

shrimp

  Faggotini with Dill, Shrimp and Zucchini, 122

  Gnocchetti with Fava Beans, Shrimp and Pistachio Pesto, 57–59

soppressata, in Grandma Rosie's Timballo, 184

Sorprese with Roasted Butternut Squash and Hazelnuts, 172

spaghetti

Ink Spaghetti alla Chitarra with Cured Yolk and Poached Egg, 145–146

Spaghetti Cacio e Pepe, 159

speck, in Herb Fettuccine with Mussels and Speck, 152

spinach

Gnocchi Verdi with Provolone Fonduta, 93

Spinach and Taleggio Rotolo, 180

Tagliatelle Primavera, 142

spray bottles, 13

squash

Butternut Squash and Roasted Pear Cappellacci with Sage, 101–102

Ratatouille Lasagna, 176

Sorprese with Roasted Butternut Squash and Hazelnuts, 172

Tagliatelle Primavera, 142

squid ink

Ink Farfalle with Octopus, Calabrian Chiles and Chickpeas, 167

Ink Spaghetti alla Chitarra with Cured Yolk and Poached Egg, 145–146

storage, 18

stracci, in Chestnut Stracci with Braised Pork Ribs and Pears, 160

Strozzapreti with Green Tomatoes and Crab, 69

summer squash

Ratatouille Lasagna, 176

Tagliatelle Primavera, 142

Sunchoke Cappelletti with Kale and Apples, 121

Sweet Pea Raviolini with Mascarpone and Mint, 112

Sweet Potato Gnocchi with Pecans and Prosciutto, 76

Swiss chard

Pizzoccheri with Swiss Chard, Fingerlings and Grana Padana, 155

Pumpkin Gnocchi with Pancetta and Swiss Chard Pesto, 75

Tagliarini with Cerignola Olives and Lemon, 156

Tagliatelle Primavera, 142

Taleggio cheese

Radicchio and Taleggio Triangoli with Pork Cheek Ragu, 116–119

Spinach and Taleggio Rotolo, 180

timballo, in Grandma Rosie's Timballo, 184

tomatoes, cherry, in Cocoa Mafaldine with Quail and Walnuts, 151

tomatoes, chopped

Ink Farfalle with Octopus, Calabrian Chiles and Chickpeas, 167

Lorighittas with Heirloom Tomatoes, 'Nduja and Oil-Cured Olives, 47–48

Maccheroni di Busa with Brasciole and Pomodoro Sauce, 54–56

Ratatouille Lasagna, 176

tomatoes, crushed

Chestnut Stracci with Braised Pork Ribs and Pears, 160

Ciciones with Lentil Stew, 60

Eggplant Cannelloni, 179

Mezzi Paccheri with Peas and Onions, 65–66

Orecchiette and Meatballs, 51–53

Pappardelle with Wild Mushroom Bolognese, 147–148

Radicchio and Taleggio Triangoli with Pork Cheek Ragu, 116–119

Ratatouille Lasagna, 176

Saffron Gnocchi with Butter Poached Lobster and Tarragon, 83–84

Spinach and Taleggio Rotolo, 180

tomatoes, green, in Strozzapreti with Green Tomatoes and Crab, 69

tomatoes, halved

Chickpea Gnudi with Heirloom Tomatoes, 90

Eggplant Mezzaluna with Tomato Confit and Pesto, 99–100

Farfalle with Roasted Tomatoes and Chile, 139–141

Tagliatelle Primavera, 142

tomato paste

Cappellacci dei Briganti with Eggplant Caponata, 164

Cocoa Mafaldine with Quail and Walnuts, 151

Malloreddus with Juniper Berry Braised Venison, 39–41

Pappardelle with Wild Mushroom Bolognese, 147–148

Radicchio and Taleggio Triangoli with Pork Cheek Ragu, 116–119

tortelli, in Pork and Parsnip Tortelli with Apples and Walnuts, 126–128

triangoli, in Radicchio and Taleggio Triangoli with Pork Cheek Ragu, 116–119

trofie, in Black Pepper Trofie with Clams, Fennel and Sausage, 45–46

truffles, in Egg Yolk Gnudi with Truffles, 72

tuna, in Herb Fazzoletti with Tuna and Castelvetrano Olives, 171

Veal Agnolotti with Mustard Greens and Pecorino, 105–106

veal, ground

Orecchiette and Meatballs, 51–53

Veal Agnolotti with Mustard Greens and Pecorino, 105–106

vegetable stock, in Ciciones with Lentil Stew, 60

venison, in Malloreddus with Juniper Berry Braised Venison, 39–41

vermouth, in Ricotta Cavatelli with Mussels, 32

walnuts

Cocoa Mafaldine with Quail and Walnuts, 151

Pork and Parsnip Tortelli with Apples and Walnuts, 126–128

water, introduction to, 14

watercress, in Sweet Pea Raviolini with Mascarpone and Mint, 112

whole wheat flour

Cecamariti with Figs, Pancetta and Brussels Sprouts, 42

introduction to, 13

Whole Wheat Cavatelli with Mushrooms and Goat Cheese Crema, 27–28

wine

Artichoke Casonsei with Hazelnuts and Goat's Milk Ricotta, 125

Black Pepper Trofie with Clams, Fennel and Sausage, 45–46

Ciciones with Lentil Stew, 60

Cocoa Mafaldine with Quail and Walnuts, 151

Eggplant Cannelloni, 179

Espresso Braised Short Rib and Celery Root Ravioli, 115

Gnocchetti with Fava Beans, Shrimp and Pistachio Pesto, 57–59

Herb Fettuccine with Mussels and Speck, 152

Herb Garganelli with Artichokes and Meyer Lemon, 163

Ink Farfalle with Octopus, Calabrian Chiles and Chickpeas, 167

Malloreddus with Juniper Berry Braised Venison, 39–41

Mint Corzetti with Lamb Sausage and Broccoli Rabe, 168

Orecchiette and Meatballs, 51–53

Pappardelle with Wild Mushroom Bolognese, 147–148

Radicchio and Taleggio Triangoli with Pork Cheek Ragu, 116–119

Ratatouille Lasagna, 176

Roasted Garlic Fettuccine with Razor Clams and Baccala, 136–138

Roasted Potato Gnocchi with Robiola, Artichokes and Capers, 85–86

Spinach and Taleggio Rotolo, 180

Whole Wheat Cavatelli with Mushrooms and Goat Cheese Crema, 27–28

zucchini

Faggotini with Dill, Shrimp and Zucchini, 122

Ratatouille Lasagna, 176

Tagliatelle Primavera, 142